AN ENCOURAGING WORD

Reflections

**Roger Prescott
and
Ronald Rude**

AN ENCOURAGING WORD

Copyright © 1983 by
The C.S.S. Publishing Company, Inc.
Lima, Ohio

All rights reserved. No portion of this book may be reproduced or utilized in any form or by any means, electronic or mechanical including photocopying, without permission in writing from the publisher. Inquiries should be addressed to: The C.S.S. Publishing Company, Inc., 628 South Main Street, Lima, Ohio 45804.

0508/ISBN 0-89536-610-X   PRINTED IN THE U.S.A.

*Just as a whole world
of beauty can be discovered
in one flower, so the
great grace of God can be
tasted in one small moment.*

— Henri Nouwen

*This is for Shirley and Nancy:
a model mother-daughter team,
who happen to be our wives, and
who bring us much stability,
encouragement and love.*

ACKNOWLEDGMENTS

Special acknowledgment is made to the following for permission to reprint selections from the books and other sources listed below.

From . . .

Adventure Inward, by Morton T. Kelsey, Augsburg Publishing House, Copyright 1980. Used by permission.

Bless My Growing, by Gerhard Frost, Augsburg Publishing House, Copyright 1974. Used by permission.

Blessed Is the Ordinary, by Gerhard Frost, Winston Press, Copyright 1980. Used by permission.

"Birthright." Reprinted by permission of Robin E. Van Cleef.

By the Still Waters, by Vance Havner. Reprinted with permission from *Dawnings — Finding God's Light in the Darkness*, edited by Phyllis Hobe, Guideposts Associations, Inc., Carmel, New York 10512.

Change of Weather, by Winfield Townley Scott. Reprinted by permission of Doubleday and Company, Inc., Copyright 1964.

Collected Poems, by Sara Teasdale. Copyright 1920 by Macmillan Publishing Company, Inc., renewed 1948 by Mamie T. Wheless.

Homing: In the Presence, by Gerhard Frost, Winston Press, Copyright 1978. Used by permission.

I Opener, by Herbert Brokering. Used by permission from Concordia Publishing House. Copyright 1974.

Looking Up . . . While Lying Down, by John E. Biegert. Copyright 1978, 1979 by John E. Biegert. Used by permission of the Pilgrim Press, 132 West 31st St., New York, New York 10001.

Lord, Could You Make It a Little Better? by Robert Raines, Word Books, Copyright 1972. Used by permission of the author.

Peace Amidst the Pieces, by Jan Markell, Adventure Publications, Copyright 1977. Used by permission.

Seasons in the Sun, Pocket Books, Division of Simon and Schuster, Copyright 1972.

"To Dance With the Waves." Reprinted by permission of Dwight H. Judy.

There Are Men Too Gentle to Live Among Wolves, by James Kavanaugh, Nash Publishing Company, Copyright 1970.

Woman to Woman, by Raphael Marie Turnbull. The C. R. Gibson Company, for excerpts from *Woman to Woman* by Raphael Marie Turnbull. Copyright 1979 by Raphael Marie Turnbull and the C. R. Gibson Company.

You Count, You Really Do, by William Miller. Copyright 1976, Augsburg Publishing House. Used by permission.

Every effort has been made to give proper credit and to gain approval for reprinting copyrighted material. If we have missed at any point, it is inadvertant and we would like to correct it in future editions. Please write to C.S.S. Publishing Company, Inc. for any corrections or additions.

PREFACE

"The real purpose of books is to
trap the mind into doing its
own thinking."
— Christopher Morley

"I am living proof that you can go
through the world on borrowed words."
— Dr. George Sheehan

The messages of this book are put together in the spirit of these two quotations. I always enjoy finding a great piece of writing and then using it in sermons, speeches, presentations, and even general letter writing. There's all sorts of good material floating around in our world, but it needs to be distilled and drawn together. If I have any talent, it seems to be in seeing what is really good, and then sorting it out and gathering it into manageable chunks for myself and others. This book contains some of those chunks.

This is a sequel to my first book, *Hello, My Friend*, published by C.S.S. in 1981. The format is similar, but I've added discussion questions to help lead to deeper thought. The format used seemed the easiest way to write it — for us — and to use it — for you. I've also added another writer/editor; a bright and sensitive young pastor who has been able to find and write about some of the meaningful things in our world. Ronald Rude, as co-author, introduces thoughts that help light up other thoughts.

With all the noise and rush of our world, the fast pace and movement of things, it is really hard to concentrate for very long. Therefore, these daily reflections have been made concise and poignant. We hope that some of them will contain a "contact" for some of your thoughts, as you carry them with you throughout the day.

Finally, friends, let us give thanks for books and thoughts which inspire us and for those who write them. We've lost the sources of many of these ideas and thoughts, but wherever possible, we have given credit. If we have missed at any point, corrections will be made in future editions.

It is easy enough to say that God is seeking us. But it is harder to realize that we need to prepare ourselves so that She can break through us, to us. Maybe this book will help us, and those with whom we share it, to do just that. So, the next time you want to reflect, or it's your turn for devotions . . . reach for this book.

Shalom,
Roger Prescott, Pastor
Director of FRIENDS
Lutheran Social Services of North Dakota
Box 389
Fargo, North Dakota 58107

PREFACE

A Chinese proverb says, "The faintest ink is better than the strongest memory." With this thought in mind, this book has been compiled.

From time to time, most of us come upon pieces of writings or hear stories that really speak to the heart. When this happens, a natural encounter of sorts takes place, and we are quickened.

But unless this gift is cut out and saved or written down and stored in some retrievable place, it becomes lost. With the passing of time, so goes the remembrance of something we found nourishing for our lives. And once the gift is lost it's almost impossible to find, especially in time for when it's needed again.

That has been my experience, anyway.

So, I have become a gatherer of the written and spoken word — thoughts, stories, poetry, illustrations, metaphors, lyrics, anything and everything that speaks to my human condition and experience. As a result, I'm on my way to accumulating a rather respectable file (eh . . . hem, I mean, pile) of good material which I use in my ministry as a parish pastor. These are writings which grab me in all my fulness and emptiness . . . and I figure if it affects me that way, a few other people might be moved, too.

This book is a collection of some of those pieces, put together with scripture, prayers, my own thoughts, and some humor.

I'm grateful to Roger Prescott for asking me to share in this book with him. Roger has been my mentor and friend for nine years now. He continues to be a source of inspiration and common sense, time and time again. Undoubtedly, much of what is good in my ministry is the result of his example and supportive friendship.

So, we offer herein a variety of creatively gathered writings for your use. May you be nourished, and may you find many encouraging words for your day.

Peace,
Ronald H. Rude, Pastor
Faith Lutheran Church
Isle, Minnesota 56342

Let's get quiet for a moment . . . as we think about some things together:

When former hostage William F. Keough, Jr. reached Weisbaden, West Germany, he found tons of letters waiting for him. Keough says he is not likely to forget one of them soon. It said: "I'm Susie Jones. I am eight-years-old. I am in the third grade, so I know what you've been through!"

Isn't that great! Isn't that fine! How spontaneous and understandable for an eight-year-old. Children brighten our world and warm our hearts.

As we think about this, read Mark 10:13-16.
"Let the children come to me, do not hinder them; for to such belongs the kingdom of God."

A question for your inner self:
What attributes do children have that we can gain nourishment from, if we strengthen them in ourselves?

Here's a prayer:
O God, make us like children . . . at least once in a while. Amen.

A final thought:
"It's easy to spot the villain in a home movie. He's running the projector!"

Thanks for sharing these moments. And until next time . . . be of good cheer. Peace, friend.

— RKP

Let's get quiet for a minute as we ponder some things.

Thomas Carlyle once wrote this confession:

"I have a natural talent for being in a hurry, which is a very bad talent."

Do you agree with him? Sometimes it seems that all the drivers of cars on the highways have a natural talent for being in a hurry. Many drive as though they had a date with death and were late for it.

But that's not the only bad kind of talent for hurry. It's bad to hurry through life so fast that we do not see or have time for . . .
— the things that grow . . .
— a deepened relation to God . . .
— the rich friendships that take time . . .
— the life of the mind . . .

Wow! Lots to ponder here. And as we do, read **Mark 6:31**.
". . . *Come away by yourselves to a lonely place, and rest a while.*"

A question for reflection:
Can you think of some "old saying" about hurrying?

Here's a prayer:
O God, may we have time for the finest things in life, that we may know the joy of your creation. Amen.

A final thought:
"The love in your heart wasn't
    put there to stay;
Love isn't love 'til you
    give it away!"

Blessings of all sorts to you!

— RKP

A little boy who played baseball came home from a game one day looking dejected. "Why the sad look, Rusty?" asked his father. "Lose the game?"

"Nope, it's not that, Dad," he explained. "I gotta play on another team."

"Were you traded?"

"No. Given."

Remember choosing teams as a youngster? Being first was always a boost for the ego. Even making the team felt good. We all need to belong and feel a part of things. But the system must seem like a monster to children who are never "chosen" and merely "left."

Recall a situation where someone got stuck with you. What were your feelings at the time?

Deuteronomy 7:7-8
> *It was not because you were more in number than any other people that the LORD set his love upon you and chose you, for you were the fewest of all peoples; but it is because the LORD loves you . . .*

Prayer:
I'm "left" sometimes, so I know how it feels. Amen.

A final thought:
> Clerk showing a bargain TV to a customer: "Another nice feature is if anything goes wrong, there's no fussing with warranties or guarantees. You just pay to have it fixed."

— RHR

Try to really let the imagery of this poem soak in.

>Boone took me for a walk today.
>>He pulled and tugged on his leash
>>until he was reminded to stop,
>>>or at least slow down.
>>He sniffed and rooted with that great
>>>wrinkled, hound head of his,
>>picking up bits of paper, chewed apples,
>>>other things
>>>>he cannot bear to pass by,
>>>dropping them easily after several steps.
>>He only picks things up
>>>as a form of acknowledgment,
>>>>recognition
>>>>of their existence.
>>Boone doesn't care to keep those things,
>>>he only means to touch them
>>>>then move on.
>>His pleasure's in the moving,
>>>rooting, sniffing, finding,
>>walking quickly
>>>but with head held down,
>>so he does not miss one single
>>>delightful
>>>>intriguing
>>>>Whiff
>>>>>of life.

>>>>— Raphael Marie Turnbull
>>>>*Woman to Woman*
>>>1979. Published by Raphael Marie Turnbull
>>>>and the C. R. Gibson Co.

We could learn from that old dog. There are many things too precious to let go unnoticed.

John 10:10
>"I came that they may have life and have it abundantly."

2 Corinthians 9:8
>And God is able to provide you with every blessing in abundance, so that you may always have enough of everything and may provide in abundance for every good work.

A prayer:
> Dear Lord, most of this world I will never see. Much of the human condition I will not experience. But at least, Lord, open me up so I will not miss the whiffs of life you blow right under my nose. Amen.

Final thought:
> A sign on a health food restaurant reads:
> "All you should eat — $3."

— RHR

Let's get quiet for a minute . . . as we think about some things:

A bishop was called to a church to receive a group of young confirmands into adult membership in the church. He asked the old question, so familiar to all who have attended such occasions. "Do you renounce the devil and all his works?" (In our new *Lutheran Book of Worship* we now ask, "Do you renounce all the forces of evil, the devil, and all his empty promises?")

The young man was so awed by having such a high official instruct him, he couldn't move and just looked at him. The bishop said again, "Do you renounce the devil and all his ways?" The lad still was silent. Finally, the bishop leaned over and whispered, "Say, 'I will,' if you will." The lad in a loud voice exclaimed, "I will if you will!"

We smile at that, but that old question is something for us to ponder today.

As we think about this, read Matthew 4:8, and around there.
Then the Devil took Jesus to a very high mountain and showed him all the kingdoms of the world, in all their greatness.

A question for your inner self:
What temptation do I need to guard against today?

Here's a prayer:
O God, I am not yet willing for you to have your way with me. But I am willing to be made willing. Amen.

A final thought:
"Starting from scratch is easier when you've got some!"

Thanks for sharing these few minutes with me. And until next time . . . . . be of good cheer. Peace.

— RKP

*Where I first read this story I cannot recall. I found my notes on it in one of my old sermons. Anyone who can help me with the proper source I will be grateful to.

Let's get quiet for a minute, as we listen to a reading by James Kavanaugh. It's called "Soft and Silent."

Everything I love is soft and silent,
  My cat, the morning, the end of the day,
Even the moon in its way.

Everything I love is soft and silent,
  The water, the forest, the snow at play,
Even the mountain in its way.

Everything I love is soft and silent,
  The sun on the sand, a rainy day,
Even the wind in its way.

Everything I love is soft and silent,
  The grass, the brook, the leaves at play,
Even you in your way.
  — *There Are Men Too Gentle to Live Among Wolves*
                                    (Nash, 1970) n.p.

As we think about this today, read Psalm 65:9-10.
  Thou visitest the earth and waterest it . . .
    Thou waterest its furrows abundantly,
    settling its ridges,
  softening it with showers,
    and blessing its growth.

A question for discussion. (optional)
  What is the softest thing you know? What memories come to mind when you think of it?

Here's a prayer:
  O God, where there is injury, bring pardon. Amen.

A final thought:
  "The reason most of us don't live within our income is because we don't consider that living!"

Thanks for sharing these few moments. Have a nourishing day and be of good cheer. Until next time . . . Peace.

— RKP

> *Listening is a rare happening among human beings. You cannot listen to the word another is speaking if you are preoccupied with your appearance or with impressing the other, or are trying to decide what you are going to say when the other stops talking, or are debating about whether what is being said is true or relevant or agreeable. Such matters have their place, but only after listening to the word as the word is being uttered.*
>
> *Listening is a primitive act of love in which a person gives himself to another's word, making himself accessible and vulnerable to that word.*
>
> — William Stringfellow

Think about how good it feels to have someone really pay attention to the struggles you're trying to express in words, and then think how foolish you feel when that person doesn't hear a word you're saying.

How we need to hear one another . . . and God.

Read Luke 4:17-21
   ". . . *Today this Scripture has been fulfilled in your hearing.*"

Prayer:
   Dear Lord, help me to be considerate and really listen to people. I mean really listen. Amen.

A final thought:
   One kind word will warm three winter months.
                              — A Japanese Proverb

— RHR

"Dad, can I walk home?" My almost five-year-old daughter was with me at the office.

"No," I said, "You're too little," and the thought left my consciousness. Minutes passed . . . a couple of phone calls, some writing, a conversation with a parishioner . . . time to think about going home.

"Angie, Angie!" I looked around. All around. She was nowhere in sight. My chest pounded, my breath fluttered, fear tugged at my stomach. Where is she?

Then, a thought. I wonder if she walked home anyway. She wouldn't do that. Well, maybe. I drove around searching and then hurried home.

"Daddy, I walked home all by myself" came her proud, wide-eyed greeting. How would you have responded?

I recalled the words of a wise parent, heard a few months before, "Don't cover up fear with anger." I could have spanked her, shouted, and warned (dared?) her never to do that again, but wiser thought prevailed.

"Angie, I was very afraid. I didn't know where you were." She saw her dad vulnerable and frightened. She was sorry she hadn't told me where she was going. We hugged as we proudly talked about her first walk home alone.

Question to ponder:
Can you think of a time when you felt lonely, rejected, helpless, or afraid, but instead of sharing that feeling honestly, you became angry at someone? Why do you think that was?

Proverbs 15:4
A gentle tongue is a tree of life,
but perverseness in it breaks the spirit.

Here's a prayer:
Dear Lord, You create feelings. They help keep us in tune with ourselves and "others." Help us not to repress, confuse, or deny those feelings. Amen.

A final thought:
Ever notice that if you think about something at three o'clock in the morning and then again at noon the next day, you get different answers?

— Charles Schultz,
creator of "Peanuts"

— RHR

Let's get quiet for a minute . . . as we think about some things together:

> A woman expressed distress because she felt she had lost her sense of God. So a friend suggested, "Pray to God and ask him to touch you. He'll do it. He'll put his hand on you." The woman began to pray and to her amazement she actually felt a hand touch her.
>
> She cried out in joy, "He *is* touching me!" Then she paused and suspiciously added, "But you know, it felt just like *your* hand."
>
> The good friend replied, "Of course. What did you think God would be using? Did you think he would reach out of the sky to touch you? He just took the hand that was nearest and he used that."*
>
> Ah! What a thought! We might be the only ones who can help someone who might cross our paths today. Let us be sensitive to any human need. God might, then, use our hands to bring his comfort or guidance to another.

Lots to ponder here. And as we do, read Isaiah 40:31.
> *They who wait for the Lord*
> *shall renew their strength,*
> *they shall mount up with wings*
>   *like eagles,*
> *they shall run and not be weary,*
>   *they shall walk and not faint.*

A question for discussion (optional):
> Can you think of a hand tool you might have used with which to help someone? Or that someone used to help you?

Here's a prayer:
> O God, use us. And let us be sensitive to how you want to use us. Amen.

A final thought:
> "At this time of year, the easiest thing to grow in the garden is . . . tired."

Thanks for sharing these moments. Until next time . . . be of good cheer. And peace, friend.

— RKP

*This thought from Reuben Youngdahl or Halford Luccock.

Let's get quiet for a moment, as we listen to this reading from Gerhard Frost.

> *Lord, I've been wondering:*
> *Why do I say I?*
> *Why must I ask why?*
> *Why is joy so close to pain?*
> *Why do I feel transparent in the presence of a child?*
> *Why am I often lonely in a crowd?*
> *Why are people so sober before a clock? And a ten dollar bill?*
> *Why am I so loud when I'm wrong? Or so fierce when I'm afraid?*
> *Why is the human face most beautiful when it is looking up?*
> *Why, in moments of crisis, do people either curse or pray?*
> *Why does prosperity drive us apart?*
> *And adversity bring us together?*
> *Why is it painful to celebrate alone?*
> *Why does my ability to ask questions*
> *exceed my capacity to receive answers?*
> *Why am I a mystery ever to myself?*
> *Lord, give me the right questions, and bless my growing.*
> — *Bless My Growing*
> (Augsburg, 1974) p. 28

As we think about this today, read 1 Samuel 3:19
> *And Samuel grew, and the Lord was with him and let none of his words fall to the ground.*

A question for discussion or inner reflection:
> Why, in moments of crisis, do people either curse or pray?

Here's a prayer:
> O God, break us open to warmth and keep us asking "why?" without desperation. Amen.

A final thought:
> "More and more these days I find myself pondering on how to reconcile my net income with my gross habits."

Thanks for sharing these few moments. Let's do it again soon. In the meantime, be of good cheer. And, peace.

— RKP

The French painter Raymond Kargere was once asked when he thought a painting was finished. He said, "When anything more you do to it will spoil it." That's a good answer.

The philospher Aristotle said, "The aim of art is to represent not the outward appearances of things, but their inward significance."

G. K. Chesterton wrote as his definition of art these words, simply, "Art is 'drawing the line somewhere.'"

Isn't it great that God has given us people who can paint, and draw and give color to our lives, and who can see the inward significance of things? How we need that, right?

Think of your favorite piece of art. Then reflect on why it seems to grip you so.

2 Corinthians 4:7
We have this treasure in earthen vessels.

Here's a prayer:
Dear Lord, thank you for artists. Amen.

A final thought:
Cats are so unpredictable. You just never know how they'll ignore you next.

— RHR

If I could say the things I feel, it wouldn't be the same.
Some things are not spoken of, some things have no name.
And tho' the words come hard to me, I say them just for you
For this is something rare for me, this feeling is so new,
you see . . .
> *I love the way you love me, love the way you smile at me*
> *I love the way you live this life we're in*
>> — from "Birthday Song" from the album *Don McLean*.
>> Written and sung by Don McLean.
>> Published by Yahweh Tunes, Inc., BMI. 1972
>> United Artists Records, Inc.
>> Los Angeles, California 90028

Maybe you know someone who just lights up your life and makes you feel beautiful. What a gift from God. And what a gift we can give to the people we meet.

Who is your best friend presently?

Roman 1:12
> . . . That we may be mutually encouraged by each other's faith, yours and mine.

Here's a prayer:
> Dear Lord, most of us don't have a real close friend; we're too busy trying to find many friends. Slow us down and bless us with one or maybe even two close friends in life. Amen.

A final thought:
> Happiness is a slice of bread . . . buttered.

— RHR

A woman who was an expert gardener was appalled to discover some large brown worms with voracious appetites busily at work on her prize grapevines. She called the county agriculture extension agent for help. "From what you tell me," he said, "they are too big for sprays to be of much help, so I suggest that you try biological control."

"And what might that be?" she asked.

"Pick them off the vines and tromp on them," he explained.

We smile at that, but sometimes our problems just really need to be *tackled* to be made rid of. That takes courage, but through the support of others, God often brings just the amount we need.

Think of the courage and tough love demonstrated by Jesus in Luke 19:45 and around there.
And he entered the temple and began to drive out those who sold . . .

Here's a prayer:
Dear Lord, some of my bad habits have been with me for so long. Maybe today, with a little effort and your help, I could change one. Amen.

Final thought:
You've told me you love me, but there's no harm in repeating it endlessly.

— RHR

Let's get quiet for a minute . . . as we think about some things together:

> Christopher Morley, one day while observing the telephone, began to think of the people who were waiting somewhere to hear some good news. There were the parents waiting anxiously for a call from a boy or girl far from home. There was the lonely young man in the city wishing that someone would call him and talk to him. There was the young woman who was waiting for the young man to announce he was coming to take her to dinner. And he says that suddenly he wished he could call them all and give some good news to each.*
>
> Well, as a preacher, this is what I have been commissioned to do. So to every woman, to every man, to every young person who is dissatisfied, my word is that God wants you to possess a better life than you have ever known, and best of all, he will help you possess it.

Lots to ponder here. And as we do, read John 10:10.
"I came that they may have life, and have it abundantly."

A question for discussion: (optional)
What is your first recollection of using a telelphone?

Here's a prayer:
O God, hear us now as we pray. Let your will be done. Amen.

A final thought:
"Travel broadens the mind, flattens the finances, and lengthens the conversation."

Thanks for sharing these thoughts with me. And until next time . . . be of good cheer. Peace, friend.

— RKP

---

*This thought from Gerald Kennedy or Halford Luccock.

Let's get quiet for a minute . . . as we listen to a reading from e. e. cummings:

> *i thank You God for most this amazing day;*
> *for the leaping greenly spirits of trees*
> *and a blue true dream of sky;*
> *and for everything*
> *which is natural which is infinite*
> *which is yes*
>
> — from *Poems 1923-1954*
> (Harcourt, Brace and World)

Lots to think about here. And as we do, read Psalm 118:24.
This is the day which the Lord has made;
let us rejoice and be glad in it.

A question for discussion (optional):
What was your favorite toy as a child? It probably gave you many happy days. Tell a little about that.

Now . . . here's a prayer:
O God, thanks for this amazing day! Amen.

A final thought:
"What this country needs is . . . a safety net for people who jump to conclusions."

Thanks for sharing these moments with me. And until next time . . . be of good cheer. Peace, friend.

— RKP

A man writes . . .

> Since we live — and often camp — along the foggy Oregon coast, it was quite a change for us when we took a camping trip into the Rocky Mountains. On our first night at Mesa Verde National Park in Colorado, the sky seemed more brilliant than we had ever seen it, and the stars were so close you felt as if you could touch them.
>
> Our three boys decided that they would put their sleeping bags out on the ground, so they could go to sleep watching the stars. We were just settling down for the night when our youngest came into the tent, dragging his sleeping bag with him.
>
> "What's the matter?" we asked. "Is it getting too cold?"
>
> "No," he answered. "I just never knew I was so small."

This story struck me because I too sometimes feel small, like that little boy. And yet when I do, I also feel a sense of peace, knowing I'm a part of something so grand and awesome as God and his world.

Think of a time when you've felt small . . .

Psalm 8:3-4
> *When I look at thy heavens, the*
>   *work of thy fingers;*
> *the moon and the stars which*
>   *thou hast established*
> *What is man that thou art mindful*
>   *of him*
> *and the son of man that thou*
>   *dost care for him?*

Here's a prayer:
> Dear Lord, Your love and power are awesome. Thank you for the peace this gives me. Amen.

A final thought:
> She or he who laughs, lasts.

                                                  — Hugh W. Philips

                                                        — RHR

Here's a reading on self-image from a contempory greeting card.

> My problems of insecurity, inferiority, frustration and depression all began with my oatmeal bowl.
>
> See, most people's oatmeal bowls had nice things written on the bottoms so when you finished all your oatmeal it would say, "Hi there, cutie," or "You are a wonderful person," or "Yes, mother loves you," or stuff like that . . . you know, nice stuff . . .
>
> When I got down to the bottom of my oatmeal bowl, it said, "All gone, dummy."

— William Miller
You Count, You Really Do
Augsburg. 1976. pp. 51-52

There seems to be much in life that raises a question mark as to our worth as human beings. Advertisements tell us many times a day that unless you have fresh breath, feed your pets moist food rather than dry, clean the spots on your goblets, call mom and dad long distance on holidays, and wear name brand jeans, you don't really care and aren't worth much.

But God knows different, and that's really what is important, isn't it? And he uses you and me to bring that person-affirming love to our neighbors.

John 15:15
". . . but I have called you friends . . ."

Prayer:
Dear Lord of life: When no one else will love and understand me, You will and do. I'm grateful. Amen.

Final thought:
The trouble with life is that it's so daily.

— RHR

Let's get quiet for a minute, as we think about some things together.

> A young man was known for his shyness with women. His friends, therefore, were amazed the day after he had met a girl at a dance when he announced that he had become engaged. In the congratulations that followed, one friend could not resist asking how it had happened.
> "Well," explained the bashful fellow, "I danced with her three times, and I couldn't think of anything else to say."
> We smile at that, but it carries a deep meaning, too. When we can't think of what to say to another person, we need to know that it's OK just to *be* there.

Lots to think about here. And as we do, read Ezekiel 3:15.
> . . . *I came to the exiles at Telabib . . . and I sat there . . . among them seven days.*

A question for discussion or inner reflection:
> Can you recall a time when you spoke and you should have been quiet?

Here's a prayer:
> O God, when we pray, sometimes we can't think of anything to say. Hear our inner heart. Amen.

A final thought:
> "Diplomacy is telling your boss he has an open mind, instead of telling him he has holes in his head."

Thanks for sharing these few moments. Let's do it again soon. In the meantime, be of good cheer . . . and peace.

— RKP

Let's get quiet for a moment . . . as we listen to this reading from Jan Markell.

> *Last week, Lord,*
> *I asked you to show me a purpose*
> *For occupying this earth.*
> *This week,*
> *You've allowed me to*
> > *lift another's burden*
> > *weep with a stumbling sister*
> > *heal the wounds of a broken spirit*
> > *say the healing words "I'm sorry"*
> > > *to a deserving soul*
> > *send a friendship card to one who*
> > > *needed encouragement*
> > *say "I forgive you" to a seeking friend*
> > *say "Thank you" at least a dozen times*
> > *limit my expectations of others*
> > *bury a grudge*
> > *and say "I love you" much more freely.*
>
> *Lord, forgive me for doubting*
> *Even a moment,*
> *That you would answer the fervent prayer*
> > *of mine,*
> *To be an instrument of thy peace! Amen*
> > > — *Peace Amidst the Pieces*
> > > (Adventure Publications, 1977) p. 61.

As we reflect on this today, read Psalm 118:1.
> *O Give thanks to the Lord,*
> > *for he is good;*
> *His steadfast love endures for ever!*

A question for discussion or to think about. (optional)
> What have I done this week to be an instrument to bring some of God's peace and nourishment to others?

Here's a prayer:
> O God, show us a purpose. Amen.

A final thought:
> "The best thing for a double chin is . . . having stout friends!"

Thanks for sharing these moments. Until next time, be of good cheer . . . and peace!

— RKP

Have you been hugged today?

What's the best cure for depression? Would you believe it's drug-free, doesn't cost a nickel, and it's even fun?

Social scientist Virginia Satir says that to cure the blues, you need twelve hugs a day from someone you love.

Satir told the 4,000 delegates to the American Orthopsychiatric Association in Toronto that "physical contact is very important." Says Satir, "Our pores are places for messages of love."

Satir added that, "four hugs a day are necessary for survival, eight for maintenance, and twelve for growth."

Matthew 8:3
And he stretched out his hand and touched him, saying, "I will; be clean."

Prayer:
I know how I need to be hugged.
There must be others out there like me.
O lord,
free my spirit
and warm my hugging. Amen.

Final thought:
A bulletin board on the lawn of a New Jersey church reads: "We reserve the right to accept everybody."

— RHR

Have you ever been in a hurricane, tornado, blackout, earthquake, or other major disaster? It can feel like the whole world is breaking apart. Everything stable and reliable seems to get sucked away. Here's a story of a minor earthquake. A man writes . . .

> The early-morning earthquake in the Los Angeles area last spring was my three-year-old grandson's first earthquake experience. The swaying of the house and the clatter of the window panes awakened him that morning. Within seconds he was in his parents' bedroom, pulling at his mom and dad and crying, "Daddy, Mommy, come quick! Someone is knocking at every door in our house."

Sometimes a problem can seem like it's knocking at us from every direction. The resulting confusion can be very frightening. We need a steady friend to help us sort the problem out.

Who is your steady friend? How did that friendship come about?

Read Luke 8:24 and around there.
And he awoke and rebuked the raging waves: and they ceased, and there was a calm.

A prayer:
Dear Lord, when everything seems to be coming at me from all directions, step into the center with me and help me see things clearly. Amen.

A final thought:
You can't change your ancestors, but you can do something about your descendants.

— RHR

Let's get quiet for a minute . . . and think about a few things:

> Some years ago, a boy involved in an automobile accident lost the power to smile. The muscles which made smiling possible were permanently destroyed. The newspaper reported that he was awarded five-thousand dollars in damages — a sum surely not too high in view of a lifetime without smiles. Just imagine never being able to smile at those you love!
>
> Diamonds can sparkle and roses radiate loveliness but humans alone can smile. And smiling is easy to do. It is reported that there are thirteen muscles used in smiling, whereas sixty-five are needed for frowning.
>
> So when you're getting dressed tomorrow morning, don't forget to put on your smile. It will increase your face value . . . and make our world a warmer place.

Lots to ponder here. And as we do, read Proverbs 15:13.
A glad heart makes a cheerful countenance . . .

A question for discussion (optional):
Think of a famous person who has a radiant smile. Can you think of more than one?

Now . . . here's a prayer:
O God, where there is despair, help us to bring hope. Amen.

A final thought:
"As you go about your living today, and find someone without a smile . . . give her one of yours!"

Thanks for taking time to share these thoughts today. Until next time . . . be of good cheer. And peace, friend.

— RKP

Let's get quiet for a minute . . . as we listen to a reading from Jan Markell.

> *Lord, how many miracles have I overlooked today?*
> *Some of the greatest are the smallest.*
> > *A snowflake*
> > *A butterfly*
> > *A colored leaf*
> > *The fragrance of a flower . . .*
> *Or, a smile from a friend,*
> > *on a mundane Monday.*
> *A card received for absolutely no occasion*
> > *other than being me.*
> *A squeeze of the hand.*
> *A wink.*
> *An arm around my shoulder.*
> *Simple things.*
> *Help me to listen to the silence, Lord,*
> *And bask in the joy of simple things . . .*
> *And the small miracles of life!*
> > — From *Peace Amidst the Pieces*
> > (Adventure Publications: Staples, Minnesota) p. 34

Lots to reflect on here. And as we do, read Psalm 46:10.
>   . . . *Be still, and know that I am God.*

A question to ponder:
> What is a small miracle you have seen recently? Share it with another person.

Here's a prayer:
> O God, Where there is sadness today . . . bring joy. Amen.

A final thought:
> "Nothing is so responsible for the good old days as . . . not remembering them very well!"

Thanks for sharing these moments. And until next time . . . be of good cheer. Peace, friend.

— RKP

Here's a story for all of you who live in a home that doesn't always run smoothly.

>A woman was at home doing some cleaning when the telephone rang. In going to answer it, she tripped on a scatter rug and, grabbing for something to hold onto, seized the telephone table. It fell over with a crash, jarring the receiver off the hook. As it fell, it hit the family dog, who leaped up, howling and barking. The woman's three-year-old son, startled by this noise, broke into loud screams.
>
>The woman mumbled some colorful words. She finally managed to pick up the receiver and lift it to her ear, just in time to hear her husband's voice on the other end say, "Nobody's said hello yet, but I'm positive I have the right number."

Psalm 107:1
O give thanks to the Lord for he is good;
for His steadfast love endures forever.

Prayer:
Dear Lord, even when everything is falling apart, you are solid and strong and dependable. Thank you. Amen.

A final thought:
Things turn out best for people who make the best of the way things turn out.

— Art Linkletter

— RHR

We could think of our self-image as a cup — empty, full, and everything in between. Here's a poem that just really grips my instincts as a parent.

> *The most valuable thing*
> > *my parents ever gave me*
> > > *was a sense of my own worth.*
>
> *It came from the security*
> > *of knowing I was wanted,*
> > *and even more important,*
> > > *appreciated after I arrived.*
>
> *It came from being loved enough*
> > *to be chastized*
> > > *whenever I forgot that*
> > > > *right and wrong*
> > > > > *are different.*
>
> *And so when I worry that I cannot give my children much*
> > *in stocks and bonds and dividends,*
> > *I remind myself that the best security*
> > > *I can provide*
> > > > *for their older lives,*
> > > *is what I give them now*
> > > > *in their younger lives . . .*
>
> *a security that will not change as the market changes.*
> > *I give them*
> > > *the sense*
> > > > *of their own worth.*
>
> > — Raphael Marie Turnbull
> > *Woman to Woman*
> > 1979. Published by Raphael Marie Turnbull and
> > The C. R. Gibson Company

Sometimes I wonder whether every person in the world doesn't at some time have problems with self-worth and self-esteem. How we need ways to build up one another.

To think further, read Proverbs 22:6.
> *Train up a child in the way he should go, and when he is old he will not depart from it.*

Prayer:
> Dear Lord, there are days when I feel low about myself, and even other voices tell me I don't measure up. For the many ways you tell me I have worth, I say "thanks." Now help me to see great worth in every other person I meet. Amen.

A final thought:
> The best thing about being young is, if you had to do it all over again, there would still be time.
> — Sandra Clarke

— RHR

Here's a story about living each moment fully . . .

One day in early fall a class of second-graders was discussing "What I Want to Be When I Grow Up." The teacher received the usual replies — "a fireman," "a nurse." Then she asked a youngster deep in thought what he would like to be some day. He looked up with a frown and replied, "I don't even know what I want to be for Halloween yet!"

We smile at that . . . But I wonder how often we do let our minds wander too much into another time, maybe in the future somewhere, and in the meantime neglect what's taking place within and around us, now.

Can you think of a time when you've "missed" what might have been a meaningful moment with someone simply because your mind and heart were someplace else?

Here's a Scripture reading for futher thought — Matthew 6:24.
"Therefore, do not be anxious about tomorrow, for tomorrow will be anxious for itself. Let the day's own trouble be sufficient for the day."

Prayer:
Dear Lord, I need hope and vision and future dreams to stretch my heart forward. But I also need, probably even more, a wide openness to live *this* day as fully as I can. Help me this day. Amen.

A final thought:
A sign in pet store window says,
> Wanted: Boy, age 9 to 11, who loves large white dogs.
> Signed: large white dog who loves boys.

— RHR

The poet Robert Frost once said: "The reason why worry kills more people than work is that more people worry than work." Here's a snippet on over-worrying.

> Ice now covers about one-tenth of the earth, raising the question of what on earth would happen if it all melted. For one thing, marine scientists tell us, the ocean would rise by as much as 200 feet, flooding New York City and leaving the Statue of Liberty waist-deep in water.
>
> The sea would flood other cities as well — among them Washington, D.C., Miami, Houston, Los Angeles and San Francisco. The city of Memphis would be on the Gulf of Mexico. The Arctic Ocean would cover a big chunk of Alaska. Hawaii's mountains would still jut out of the ocean, but the state's coastal cities would be under-water.
>
> There's no need to panic, however. Most scientists say the ice won't start melting for several thousand years — or perhaps even longer.

Matthew 6:25
"Therefore I tell you, Do not be anxious about your life . . ."

Matthew 6:34
". . . Let the day's own trouble be sufficient for the day."

Here's a prayer:
Dear Lord, sometimes I worry long before worrying could possibly do any good. Forgive me for wasted time and energy. Help me to live today fully. Amen.

A final thought:
It's good to remember that the tea kettle, though it's up to its neck in hot water, continues to sing.

— RHR

Let's get quiet for a minute . . . as we think about some things together:

> I think it was President Woodrow Wilson who is credited with this limerick:
>
> > *For beauty I am not a star,*
> > *There are others more handsome, by far;*
> > *But my face, I don't mind it*
> > *Because I'm behind it,*
> > *The folks at my front get the jar.*
>
> It sounds like he enjoyed being himself . . . a lesson we all need to learn.
> Very few of us dare to be ourselves. We try to walk, talk and think like others, especially those we admire. Yet the secret of being loved and appreciated is naturalness . . . the willingness to be "just plain me." So let's wrap up all our strengths, all our weaknesses, our successes and our failures, and take the package "for better or worse." We'll get farther and get there faster than if we are stopping all the time to change our identity. As someone has said, "Why be a smudgy carbon copy of someone else when we can be a clear original of ourselves?"

Lots to ponder here. And as we do, read Psalm 139:14.
> . . . *Thou knowest me right well.*

A question for discussion (optional).
> Describe an old shirt, jacket, or other piece of clothing you love to wear . . . that makes you feel like "yourself."

Here's a prayer:
> O God, lay hold upon our strengths, and give us wings! Amen.

A final thought:
> "Fifty years ago, when people finished a day's work, they needed rest. Today we need exercise."

Thanks for sharing these moments with me. And until next time . . be of good cheer. Peace, friend.

— RKP

Let's get quiet for a minute . . . as we listen to a reading from Gerhard Frost. *Bless My Growing* (Augsburg, 1974) p. 63.

> *"Yes, doubt does keep gnawing*
> *at one's faith."*
> *I said it to a friend,*
> *my friend in deep distress.*
> *I said it to encourage,*
> *but quickly he replied,*
> *without a moment's hesitation,*
> *"But faith keeps gnawing*
> *at our doubts, too!"*
>
> *It was a great response.*
> *I am strengthened by it.*
> *Intending to comfort,*
> *I was comforted.*
> *Today I walk more boldly*
> *as I say:*
> *Yes, doubt does gnaw at my faith,*
> *but faith gnaws, too,*
> *and faith has better teeth!*

As we think about this today, read Mark 9:24.
". . . I believe; help my unbelief!"

A question for discussion or our inner self. (optional)
Doubt and faith have been called opposites. But really, indifference is the opposite of faith. Is this true?

Here's a prayer:
O God, we do believe. But help our unbelief. Amen.

A final thought:
Did you ever think of this? . . . It is also true that the early worm is gotten by the bird.

Thanks for taking time to share these thoughts today. Until next time . . . be of good cheer. And peace, friend.

— RKP

Instructions do not always make life as simple as we would like to think. George MacLeod tells of a journey he made in India some years ago. He saw in a railroad station a wooden crate labeled for shipment and marked, *This case should be carried bottom upward.* So far, so good! But it was further labeled, *The top is marked bottom to avoid confusion.*

— Alexander Miller

We smile at that, but life can be that confusing, can't it? And often our feeble and human attempts to straighten things out just lead to more confusion. We need help from God.

Isaiah 40:8
The grass withers, the flower fades; but the word of our God will stand for ever.

Prayer:
Dear Lord,
When a problem baffles me
day after day
keeping me in a rut, making
my life less than it could be,
Enable me to seek your help
and the help of a qualified person.
Then . . .
give me a trusting spirit. Amen.

A final thought:
The three most commonly told lies in this country are: "Gee, you haven't changed a bit," "I never got the message," and "I put that check in the mail to you yesterday."

— RHR

Here's part of a song to help us think about how good it is to be visited by someone whom we love, and how important it is for us to visit the lonely.

> *". . . that afternoon, we spent the day*
> *with Uncle Frank, remember,*
> *and his wife, Auntie May,*
> *well do you know, since then*
> *I've received up to four letters*
> *all of which repeat the same*
> *they say thrilled to bits*
> *can't believe you came*
> *we've relived it both*
> *over time and time again*
> *and if there's ever a chance*
> *or even half*
> *you might be our way, oh*
> *would you promise to stay*
> *we will . . ."*
>
> — From "We Will" composed by Ray O'Sullivan.
> Sung by Gilbert O'Sullivan on the album
> *Gilbert O'Sullivan Himself,* 1972.
> London Records, Inc.
> 539 West 25th Street, New York, New York 10001

Wow! Powerful. It's amazing how a timely visit or even an encouraging letter can sometimes be just the needed thing for both parties.

Matthew 25:36
  "I was sick and you visited me . . ."

Prayer:
  Dear Lord, when I needed a friend, you sent someone. Now send me. Amen.

Final thought:
  What you think might mean something to me just like your something might mean nothing to me, only I would never say to you your nothing is nothing, 'cuz to you it's something.

— Edith Bunker

—RHR

Here's something to ponder today:

There's a reading that speaks to many people and seems to be good advice for us all. Ann Landers quoted it in one of her columns recently. I believe she found it in an Al-Anon book:

Today is mine. It is unique. Nobody in the world has one exactly like it. It holds the sum of all my past experiences and all my future potential. I can fill it with joyous memories or ruin it with fruitless worry. If painful recollections of the past come into mind, or frightening thoughts of the future, I can put them away. They cannot spoil today for me. It is mine.
— Anonymous

Lots to think about here. And as we do, read Psalm 118:24.
This is the day which the Lord has made; let us rejoice and be glad in it.

A question for reflection and discussion:
Why do you think it is that we have so much trouble experiencing the wonder of each day . . . each moment?

Here's a prayer:
O God, thanks for helping us live each day with good cheer. Amen.

A final thought:
If we could cross poison ivy with four-leaf clovers . . . **maybe** we'd have a rash of good luck.

Be careful today.

— RKP

Let's get quiet for a minute, as we listen to a reading from Gerhard Frost. It's called "His Way for Me."

> *The profoundest thing*
> *one can say of a river*
> *is that it's on its way to the sea.*
>
> *The deepest thought*
> *one can think of a person*
> *is that he or she is a citizen of eternity.*
>
> *Moments and years,*
> *years and moments,*
> *pass like sea bent streams.*
> *And I? I'm carried by the current*
> *of an all-possessing Love.*
> *I'm on my way, God's way for me,*
> *so let it be.*
>
> — *Blessed Is the Ordinary*
> (Winston Press, 1980) p. 9

Lots to ponder here. And as we do, read John 14:1-2.
"Let not your hearts be troubled; believe in God, believe also in me. In my Father's house are many rooms; if it were not so, would I have told you that I go to prepare a place for you?"

A question for discussion. (optional)
When you think of a river, which one comes to your mind? Tell something of your relationship with that river.

Here's a prayer:
O God, help keep us centered in the current of your love. Amen.

A final thought:
"They're not really fixin' the streets. They're just movin' the holes so the motorists can't memorize 'em."
— Herb Shriner

Thanks for sharing these thoughts. Be of good cheer. Until next time . . . peace.

— RKP

There's a bumper sticker which reads, "If life deals you a lemon, make lemonade!" Good words, aren't they? The following story captures that spirit even more. A man writes . . .

> When I declined to join my wife in a wallpaper hanging project, she went ahead with it by herself. I came home from work one day and found a mess. My wife was sprawled on the floor, tangled in a collapsed ladder, swathed in wallpaper and garnished with paste. She was mad. "Don't move!" I shouted as I ran for the camera.
> I took her picture titled "Wrapsody in Glue" and sent it off to a photo contest. A few weeks later, we found it won first place, and the prize money covered the cost of hiring a paperhanger to do the job.
> — V. L. Newell

Yes, most problems can often be handled with a little ingenuity and a sense of the humorous. We needn't let everyday misfortunes drag us down the descending spiral of self-pity and resentment.

Today, try to think of a time when you've over-reacted to a "major" problem . . . Then, smile at yourself. Feel better?

Along with this, listen to the words of Proverbs 8:1.
> *Does not wisdom call*
> *does not understanding raise her voice?*

Prayer:
> Dear Lord, awful problems plague our world, and even my life at times. Thank you that I can keep a sense of humor at least through some of them. Amen.

A final thought:
> If you wish to travel back in time, music is the sweetest and most gentle of all roads.

— RHR

Lets get quiet for a minute . . . as we listen to this piece from Norm Shockley.* It's called *Our Rose Died Last Night*.

> *It was a big white rose, right*
> *   outside our kitchen window.*
> *Every morning it nodded to me*
> *   over my morning coffee.*
> *It handled wind and cold rains*
> *   and night frosts.*
> *I was surprised each time to*
> *   see it nodding in the*
> *morning breezes after*
> *   fighting gamely through*
> *   another night of*
> *   freezing temperatures.*
>
> *But this morning it was dead.*
> *   Last night's cold was too*
> *much, even for our morning rose.*
> *   But down at its roots*
> *in the heart of the earth the*
> *   mystery of its promise lives.*
> *   And next year one of its*
> *cousins will nod to me through*
> *   the windows some morning.*
> *Strange that God of*
> *   galaxies should bother.*

Wow! Lots to reflect on here. And as we do, read Ecclesiastes 3:1.
For everything there is a season, and a time for every matter under heaven.

A question for discussion, or to think about. (optional)
Do you have a favorite plant, tree or bush? Tell us about it.

Here's a prayer:
O God, each day, with all its miracles, is your special gift to us. Thanks. Amen.

---

*The source and origin of this piece is lost. I would be grateful to anyone who could let me know where it was published. RP

A final thought:
> "Almost every child would learn to write sooner if allowed to do her homework on wet cement."

Thanks for sharing these moments. Until next time, be of good cheer . . . and peace!

— RKP

Sometimes our lifestyles and routines need to be cracked open a little to allow some light to get in and growth to take place. Ouch! That can hurt, can't it? But there doesn't seem to be any other way.

Here's a reading by Vance Havner that carries that thought further.

Broken Things

> God uses broken things. It takes broken soil to produce a crop, broken clouds to give rain, broken grain to give bread, broken bread to give strength. It is the broken alabaster box that gives forth perfume . . . It is Peter, weeping bitterly, who returns to greater power than ever.
>
> — Vance Havner
> From *Dawnings*, edited by Phyllis Hobe
> Published by Guideposts Associates, Inc. 1981. p. 37

Question for discussion:
Think of a shattering experience that you have survived and even been strengthened from.

Mark 14:72
   . . . And he (Peter) broke down and wept.

Acts 3:6
   But Peter said, "I have no silver and gold, but I give you what I have; in the name of Jesus Christ of Nazareth, walk."

Prayer:
   Dear Lord, when some dream of mine shatters, help me to keep going. Amen.

A final thought:
   Driver at a roadside phonebooth: "Operator, could you trace this call and tell me where I am?"

— RHR

Let's get quiet for a minute, as we ponder this piece by Jan Markell.

Slow down, world!
Halt your maddening pace
   to and fro
Going nowhere,
on the move
Yet directionless;
Running
Frantic
Pursuing elusive goals,
And leaving in the dust
A needy soul
Who wanted just 10 minutes
   of your time
To listen.
Can't you hear the deafening roar
Of humanity
In need of just one person
Who will forsake the pursuit
Of fun and games
And say,
By listening,
"I love you."

— *Peace Amidst the Pieces*
(Adventure Publications
Staples, Minnesota, 1977) p. 7

Lots to think about here. And as we do, read Psalm 46:10.
   Be still, and know that I am God.

A question for discussion or inner reflection. (optional)
   What part of your life makes you feel the most hurried? What part makes you feel the most serene?

Here's a prayer:
   O God, help us shift into the right gear at the right time. Amen.

A final thought:
   "The three stages of life are: Youth, middle-age, and 'You're looking great!'"

Thanks for sharing these few moments. Let's do it again soon. In the meantime, be of good cheer . . . and peace.

— RKP

A man writes . . .

> When we were children, my seven-year-old brother would always take me along on his bicycle. His favorite pastime was to go racing down a steep mountain road at top speed. Frightened stiff, I would close my eyes tight but never say a word for fear I would not be taken along again. Twenty years later, when we drove down that same road in a car, I asked my brother, "Do you remember how we used to ride down here on your bike? I was so scared that I always closed my eyes."
> "What!" he exclaimed, astonished. "You too?"

Fear, if we're too proud to share it, may make us blind and hardened to reality. But a fear shared with another human being is a fear cracked open and diffused. Once shared, the fear becomes receptive to the light of courage and hope.

Proverbs 29:25
> *The fear of man lays a snare,*
> *but he who trusts in the Lord is safe.*

Prayer:
> Dear Lord, no one is as courageous as I pretend to be. It's not human. Help me to face and share some of my fears. Amen.

A final thought:
> One thing that happens only once in a lifetime is you.

— RHR

Mac Davis sang a song a while back called "You've Got to Stop, and Smell the Roses." That isn't one of the chores of life, but rather one of life's rewards.

William Bengtson is a sensitive poet and friend of mine from Bronx, New York. Hear his warm and inviting words in a poem called "Last Chance."

> *when you cross that field*
> *today*
> *the one that borders just beyond*
> *your backyard fence*
>
> *when you walk that way*
> *through some special call of the sun*
>
> *or because of an unknown wild woodnote*
> *crowding you with curiosity*
>
> *linger longer than intended*
>
> *taste the texture of the day*
>
> *taste the air*
> *tape the sounds*
> *preserve the scents*
> *in some secret sachet*
> *closeted beneath your shirt*
> *make a memory-print*
> *as indelible as those*
> *of cherished childhood jaunts*
>
> *it will probably be a chance of a lifetime.*

Along with this read Psalm 19:1.
The heavens are telling the glory of God;
and the firmament proclaims his handiwork.

Prayer:
Dear Lord, help me to slow down, notice, and relish the beauty of this earth. Amen.

Final thought:
Affluence reaches equilibrium when a person spends all his leisure time repairing labor-saving devices.

— RHR

Little Jane, just out of bed one morning, was crying as though her heart would break. Her mother came hurrying to ask, "Jane, what in the world is the matter?" Sobbing, she answered, "I was just thinking, I'll have to put on my clothes every day as long as I live."

This reminds me of a phrase I heard someone say once, "The trouble with life is that it's so daily."

If we look at life in terms of its daily chores, it can seem pretty overwhelming. But if we remain open to its surprises and blessings, it can start getting rather exciting.

Along with this read Matthew 25:29.
> "For to every one who has will more be given, and he will have abundance; but from him who has not, even what he has will be taken away."

Prayer:
Dear Lord, help me not to let my daily chores get in the way of important things. Amen.

A final thought:
A For-Sale sign read:
> Unicycle — Still wild and untamed. Mounted, but never ridden.

— RHR

Let's get quiet for a moment, as we attend to this reading from Stella Halsten Hohncke. She is ninety years old this year.

> *I remember the days of my childhood,*
> *When clothing was made from a sack,*
> *With "Miller's Delight" on the front side*
> *And "Certain to Bake" on the back.*
>
> *No silk or rayon in our budget,*
> *We washed the flour sacks clean*
> *And made petticoats, pants and pajamas*
> *All worn with an air of a queen.*
>
> *For those were the days of our childhood,*
> *When things were simple and sure,*
> *Deep-rooted as our convictions*
> *And clothing was made to endure.*
>
> *I like to remember those old days*
> *When clothing was made from a sack,*
> *With "Miller's Delight" on the front side*
> *And "Certain to Bake" on the back.* *

As we think about this today, read Ecclesiastes 12:1.
   Remember also your Creator in the days of your youth . . .

A question for reflection and discussion:
   Do you recall any article of clothing you wore as a child? Tell about it. Why do you suppose you remember it?

Here's a prayer:
   O God, thank you for warm and good clothes to protect us and to bring us brightness. Amen.

A final thought:
   "The beauty of a blanket of snow is best appreciated by people with short driveways."

Take good care of yourself. You're important!

---

*From a private notebook (unpublished). Used by permission of the author.

Let's get quiet for a minute . . . as we listen to a reading from Dinah Maria Mulock Craik.*

> Oh, the comfort, the inexpressible comfort of feeling safe with a person; having neither to weigh thoughts nor measure words, but to pour them all out, just as they are, chaff and grain together, knowing that a faithful hand will take and sift them, keep what is worth keeping, and then, with the breath of kindness, blow the rest away.

Beautiful! Lots to ponder here. And as we do, read James 2:23. *Abraham believed God, and it was reckoned to him as righteousness; and he was called the friend of God.*

A question for discussion or for your inner self. (optional)
Recall a person with whom you could share your innermost thoughts.

Here's a prayer:
O God, thank you for friends who accept us as we are. Amen.

A final thought:
"If life were a bed of roses, some people wouldn't be happy until they developed an allergy."

Thanks for sharing these few moments with me. And until next time . . . . be of good cheer. Peace, friend.

— RKP

---

*Found on a banner in a church in North Dakota.

Helen Keller once said:

> I asked a friend who had just returned from a long walk in the woods what she had observed. "Nothing in particular," she replied.
>
> How was that possible, I asked myself. I who cannot hear or see, find hundreds of things to interest me through mere touch. I feel the delicate symmetry of a leaf. I pass my hands lovingly about the rough shaggy bark of a pine. Occasionally, if I am very fortunate, I place my hand gently on a small tree and feel the happy quiver of a bird in full song.

What a sensitive human being! How the world has been blessed by this woman.

As we think about this, read Isaiah 5:12.
> They have lyre and harp,
>   timbrel and flute and wine at their feasts
> but they do not regard the deeds of the Lord
>   or see the work of his hands.

Here's a prayer:
> Dear Lord, keep me from wasting half my life not *really* seeing much of anything. Amen.

A final thought:
> Old-timer to a friend: What I don't understand is how I got over the hill, without ever being on top.

— RHR

*Once there was a boy
who liked cracking rocks.
He always thought
how he was the first to see
the inside of the rock.
He opened thousands of them.
When he was older,
he waited for the sun
to rise.
In the winter
he was the first to walk
across the new snow.
Now he is a morning milkman
He still likes to crack things open.*

— Herbert Brokering
"I" Opener
Concordia Publishing, 1974. p. 15

Sounds like a person who likes surprises, doesn't it? What a great attitude for getting the most out of life.

Recall a time when you got up real early. Can you remember the sounds and smells and purpose?

Isaiah 42:9
Behold, the former things have come to pass, and new things I now declare; before they spring forth I tell you of them.

Here's a prayer:
Dear Lord, thank you for those times when circumstances or my own energies get me up at the crack of dawn. Amen.

A final thought:
As humans, we need recognition. Like the little boy who says, "Grandma, let's play darts. I'll throw the darts and you say 'Wonderful.'"

— RHR

My wife, Nancy, and I were just arriving at a movie theater one evening when we noticed two cars simultaneously heading for the same parking spot. Almost instantly, the cars screeched to a halt and both drivers bolted from their vehicles. Shouting, and their bodies set in a "you want to fight about it?" stance, they began a heated argument. You can imagine the scene. One man even took off his sportcoat, apparently wanting to demonstrate in a vivid way his resolve.

We weren't able to stick around long enough to see how things were worked out. But I've often thought about that scene . . . so spontaneous and explosive. What had or was happening in their lives to bring about such quickfisted anger? Where had they learned to trust this method of resolving conflicts?

— Ronald Rude

A thought to ponder:
Recall a fist-fight you have witnessed. Can you remember the atmosphere?

Genesis 4:8
And when they were in the field, Cain rose up against his brother Abel, and killed him.

Here's a prayer:
O god of peace, give us good ways of handling our most intense and often potentially dangerous feelings. Amen.

A final thought:
There's a stream of goodness in life. Try to get into it.

— RHR

Let's get quiet for a minute . . . as we think about some things together:

> There is a beautiful promise of God in the 121st Psalm.
> "The Lord will keep your going out and your coming in from this time forth and for evermore."
>
> This is a large part of life, isn't it? Think of all the "going out" in our lives: going out to work in the morning, or perhaps at times to look for work; going out to school, to the market, to church. In our "going out" we are usually strong. Then there's the "coming in." Tired, perhaps, after a hard day's work, or a tough meeting, perhaps a disappointment, but "coming in" to rest.
>
> Claim this great promise. "The Lord will keep your going out and your coming in . . ." It's a way of remembering we're always in his hand.

As we ponder this today, read Psalm 121:8.
The Lord will keep your going out and your coming in from this time forth and for evermore.

A question for discussion (optional).
Can you recall a "special" doorway in your life?

Here's a prayer:
O God, in all the part of life . . . morning and evening . . . far and near . . . night and day . . . may we walk with you. Amen.

A final thought:
"A grandmother is a baby sitter who doesn't hang around the refrigerator!"

Thanks for sharing these moments. Until next time . . . be of good cheer. Peace, friend.

— RKP

Let's get quiet for a minute, as we listen to a reflective prayer by Jan Markell. It's called *Be Patient With Us Lord.*

> *Lord, you must feel like*
> *Washing your hands of us some days.*
> *Do you ever tire of*
> > *shaking fists*
> > *defiant rebellion*
> > *indifference*
> > *and having your love spurned?*
> *Do you ever want to let the ship go down*
> *And let us fend for ourselves?*
>
> *Great God, how we need you!*
> *Not just to salvage the wreckage,*
> *But to rebuild broken spirits,*
> *To remind us that You put it all together, once,*
> *and that You again have the healing balm*
> > *to mend lives,*
> > *give meaning to chaos,*
> > *purpose to the routine*
> > *goals to the directionless*
> > *order to the confusion*
> > *love amidst animosity*
> > *and to provide joy and thanksgiving*
> > *in the mire of apathy and boredom.*
> *Be patient with us, Lord.*
> *Remind us of our dependence . . .*
> > *our utter weakness and inability*
> > > *to make it on our own. Amen.*
>
> — *Peace Amidst the Pieces*
> (Adventure, 1977) p. 59

Lots to think about here. And as we do, read Psalm 46:1.
> God is our refuge and strength, a very present help in trouble.

A question for discussion. (optional)
> Can you think of a time when God did seem to be really patient with you?

Here's a small prayer.
> O God, yes, be patient with us. Amen.

A final thought. Actually a question:
"How old would you think you were, if you didn't know how old you were?"

— RKP

A mother brought her two preschool children to visit their eighty-six-year-old grandmother. Such visits were always a production. Grandma lived in a small mobile home, and the kids usually managed to wreak havoc on it. During one particularly rambunctious visit, after picking up after the kids all morning long, the mother finally bellowed, "Would you two please stop throwing everything on the floor! Don't you know cleanliness is next to . . ."

"Loneliness," interrupted Grandma, looking at the mess with bright eyes. "Cleanliness is next to loneliness."

How we need children in this old world. They help to keep us centered more than anything. We need wise grandmas and grandpas, too.

Reflect on the wisdom you've received from both ends of the age spectrum.

Mark 10:14
"Let the children come to me . . ."

Prayer:
Dear Lord, keep me from being so clean and well-kept that I cease to be human. Also, thanks for fresh insights and tried ways. Amen.

Final thought:
Experience is a wonderful thing. It enables you to recognize a mistake when you make it again.

— RHR

Let's get quiet for a moment, as we listen to a little piece from Raymond J. Council:*

> *May things of joy, beauty,*
> *   truth, and love*
> *BLOOM in your life.*
>
> *And if not bloom,*
> *   Then SPROUT*
>
> *And if not sprout,*
> *   Then TAKE ROOT.*
>
> *And if not take root,*
> *   Then BE SOWN.*

Much to think about here. And as we do, read Matthew 13:18-23. *"Hear then the parable of the sower . . ."*

A question for discussion (optional):
    What things of joy or beauty have sprouted or bloomed in your life recently?

Here's a prayer:
    O God, help us to accept each other . . . wherever we are in our growth. Amen.

A final thought:
    "One good thing about food costs going up . . . Everyday there's an announcement that the stuff is bad for you anyway."

Thanks for sharing these few moments with me. And until next time . . . be of good cheer. Peace.

                                                              — RKP

---

*This was spotted on a church banner.

Let's get quiet for a minute . . . as we ponder some things.

> Remember that beautiful little prayer that many children pray each night?
> *Now I lay me down to sleep,*
> *I pray the Lord my soul to keep.*
> *If I should die before I wake,*
> *I pray the Lord my soul to take.*
>
> Karen Langford Brown, a poet from Louisiana, suggests one for awakening. It goes like this:
>
> *As I waken from my sleep,*
> *This brand new day of Yours I greet.*
> *Safe You've kept me through the night*
> *I'll serve you now with all my might.*
>
> I like that! Even better than the one for night. Why not try it tomorrow?

Lots to think about here. And as we do, read Psalm 118:24.
This is the day which the Lord has made;
Let us rejoice and be glad in it.

A question for discussion (optional):
What prayers do you recall from your childhood? For bedtime, mealtime, othertime?

Now . . . here's a prayer:
O God, I want to be close to you . . . Night and day. Amen.

A final thought:
"You know you are in a small town when you can't walk for exercise because every car that passes you offers you a ride."

Thanks for sharing these moments with me. And until next time . . . be of good cheer. Peace, friend.

— RKP

Here's a poem by William Bengtson showing how desperately, deep down, we all need to feel loved.

> *You must tell me*
> *that you love me*
>
> *spell it out*
> *in whispered italics*
>
> *say it over slow*
> *and slower yet*
> *with much mouthing*
>
> *as one would*
> *to a pre-schooler*
> *to be sure I've got your drift*
>
> *flash me the message*
> *by blinks*
> *of your Aldis lamp eyes*
> *or by the unmistakable meaning*
> *in the semaphore*
> *of your open arms*
>
> *each time I look at you*
> *I'm numb with disbelief*
>
> *you must tell me*
> *that you love me.*
>
> — William Bengtson

Maybe that need isn't even down that deep, but rather on the tip of our tongues, waiting to be blurted out.

Read John 21:15 and around there:
"*Simon, son of John, do you love me more than these?*"

Prayer:
O God, help me not to hold back on those warm impulses in me that want to tell and show people I love them. Maybe that's one way you let others know of your love. Amen.

A final thought:
A Dallas music company ad reads: "Rent a toot or buy a tweet, boom, zing, twang, tinkle, hum or plink."

— RHR

> The little three-year-old was thrilled as she came upon the low drinking fountain in the shopping mall. "Hey, this is just my age," she shouted and giggled. "This is just my age!"

Wow! How good it is to come upon anything that fits like a glove our particular stage and need in life, whether you're three or thirty-three or ninety-three. Something deep inside of us appreciates anything that makes a connection with who we are. It might be a song, a story, or even a drinking fountain.

In light of this, read again these words from John 6:67-68.
Jesus said to the twelve, "Will you also go away?" Simon Peter answered him, "Lord, to whom shall we go? You have the words of eternal life . . ."

Here's a prayer:
Thank you, O God, for the things that speak to me and for people who seem to know my need of the moment. Amen.

A final thought:
After all is said and done, there's usually a lot more said than done.

— RHR

Anatole France once wrote, "What is traveling? Changing your place? By no means. Traveling is changing your opinion and your prejudice." The following poem captures the adventurous spirit of really traveling.

> "I wonder where that road goes?"
>   His need to know
>   has filled my life
>   up to the brim!
> My memories are full
>   of big green meadows
>   that suddenly appear around a bend,
>   or rocky canyons
>   we never dreamed were there.
> "I wonder where that road goes?"
>   True, often those roads
>   dwindle into nothing,
>   like plans and dreams that never quite come true.
>   But the times we find the treasures
>   are more than worth the times
>   we must turn back.
> I'm glad I found a man
>   who's not afraid to turn off from the mainstream
>   now and then,
>   because he needs to know where that road goes.
>   — Raphael Marie Turnbull
>   *Woman to Woman*
>   1979. Published by Raphael Marie Turnbull and
>   the C. R. Gibson Company.

It's funny how God will speak to us in a powerful way, when we've dared to break out of our routine. In the Bible reading today, Jesus leaves his territory and something unexpectedly marvelous happens.

Matthew 15:21-28:
>   Jesus leaves his own territory. It proves to be a great day for the woman, and I suspect, for him, too.

Prayer:
>   Dear Lord, when you call me to walk an unknown road or to meet a stranger, help me not to shiver in fright but to warmly faithfully move ahead. Amen.

A final thought:
 It's true that as humans we do not live by bread alone. We all need to be buttered up now and then.

— RHR

Let's get quiet for a minute as we ponder these words from Phillips Brooks:

Do not pray for easy lives;
Pray to be stronger people!

Do not pray for tasks equal to your powers;
Pray for powers equal to your tasks.

Then the doing of your work shall be no miracle,
*but **you** shall be a miracle.*

Every day you shall wonder at yourself, at the
  richness of life which has come to you
    by the grace of God.

Lots to think about here. And as we do, read John 10:10.
  "I have come that you might have life,
  and have it abundantly." (Jesus)

A question for some discussion. (optional)
  How would you describe "Miracle?"

Here's a prayer:
  O God, thanks for life! Amen.

A final thought:
  "Collecting anything on purpose sure seems silly . . . when you see how easily things collect by themselves!"

Hey! Thanks for sharing these few moments. Until next time, be of good cheer. And peace, Friend.

— RKP

Let's get quiet for a minute . . . as we listen to a reading from Stella Hohncke. She put these words together after a friend had died:

> *Our friend is gone*
> *   and for a voice we listen,*
> *And long to feel the handclasp*
> *   that we knew.*
> *But all in vain*
> *   there is a haunting silence,*
> *Bereft, we mourn as only friends can do.*
>
> *Our friend is gone*
> *   and we who follow after,*
> *Will feel an emptiness*
> *   the whole day long.*
> *There is a loneliness*
> *   in our remembering.*
> *We grieving, only know*
> *   our friend is gone.* *

And as we think about this today, read John 14:1.
"Let not your hearts be troubled; believe in God, believe also in me."

A question for discussion (optional):
Do you recall an object you once lost? (Like a knife, a book, a necklace) Describe the object, and then describe how you felt.

Here's a prayer:
O God, it's tough to lose a good friend. Wrap your arms of love around us to soften the blow. Amen.

A final thought:
"A calendar goes in one year, and out the other."

Thanks for sharing these moments. Until next time . . . be of good cheer. Peace, friend.

— RKP

---

*From a private notebook (unpublished). Used by permission of the author.

I wrote this poem while looking at an old photograph of Nancy, my wife, when she was three years old.

For over a decade now, I've known you
and our lives have been shaped
in a different way
because of our loving
But, you were someone long before
our paths joined
the little girl
pictured here
barefoot, sitting in the grass
next to the dirt
Your face speaks joy
wonder
insecurity
security

I'm discovering the child in you
thru pictures
stories
our own two daughters

Thank you for your love, love
How I want to grow and grow old
by your side.

— Ronald Rude

Proverbs 5:18-19
Let your fountain be blessed,
and rejoice in the wife of your
youth
a lovely hind, a graceful doe.
Let her affection fill you at all times
with delight,
be infatuated always with her love.

Prayer:
Dear Lord, thank you for my marriage partner. How I delight in her accomplishments and being. Amen.

A final thought:
Sometimes in the tiny moments of life, light suddenly is shed on our whole existence.

— James Joyce

— RHR

When life gets tough, sometimes it's good to hear some Shakespeare.

> *Sweet are the uses of adversity,*
> *Which, like the toad, ugly and venomous,*
> *Wears yet a precious jewel in his head;*
> *And this our life, exempt from public haunt,*
> *Finds tongues in trees, books in the running brooks,*
> *Sermons in stones, and good in everything.*

Lots to ponder here. And as we do, read Romans 8:28.
> *We know that in everything God works for good with those who love him, who are called according to his purpose.*

A question for some discussion. (optional)
> Has there been a time in your life when adversity has helped you grow? Would you want to go through such a time again?

Here's a prayer:
> O God, help us to see . . . really see . . . the good in all things. Amen.

A final thought:
> "There are three ways to get something done: do it yourself, hire someone to do it, or forbid your kids to do it!"

Thanks for sharing these thoughts and moments. And until next time . . . be of good cheer. Shalom, Friend.

— RKP

Let's get quiet for a moment, as we think about some things.

Peter Marshall tells us there is beauty in ordinary things which many people have never seen. For example . . .

— *Sunlight through a jar of peach-plum jelly . . .*
— *A rainbow in soapsuds in dishwater . . .*
— *An egg yolk in a blue bowl . . .*
— *White ruffled curtains sifting moonlight . . .*
— *The color of cranberry glass . . .*
— *A little cottage with blue shutters . . .*
— *Crimson roses in an old stone crock . . .*
— *The smell of newly baked bread . . .*
— *Candlelight on old brass . . .*
— *The soft brown of a cocker's eyes . . .* *

Wow! Just beautiful. And as we ponder these things, read Psalm 24:1.
The earth is the Lord's and the fulness thereof . . .

A question for reflection:
What is an "ordinary thing" that gives you a glimpse of God's beauty?

Here's a prayer:
O God, thanks for all the ordinary things around us. Help us to slow down and see them. Amen.

A final thought:
"Didja ever notice . . . No matter how much cats fight . . . there are always plenty of kittens?"

I hope your day will be filled with every good thing!

— RKP

*Found on a banner in a Minnesota Retreat Center

I know a man who is always grouchy. I'd like to talk with him about it some day, but I haven't yet.

> A waitress was trying hard to win over a stern old woman, but met resistance at every turn. At the end of the meal, she brought the check, smiled sweetly and said, "Have a nice weekend!" But the woman was implacable. "I'm afraid," she snapped, "I've made other plans."

* * * * * *

> Aunt Ana and Jennie had not spoken to each other for decades, yet when Jennie died Aunt Ana was among the first to pay her respects. Afterward I blurted out, "Aunt Ana, why did you go to Jennie's funeral when you haven't spoken to her for 20 years?"
> As quick as a flash and with her customary spunk, she shot back, "And I didn't speak to her today, either."

It's easy to see other people's destructive resentments. It's harder to see our own. Resentment means to feel over and over and over again *(re-sentire)*. Along with self-pity, it's one of our most crippling emotions.

Job 18:4
You who tear yourself in your anger . . .

Prayer:
Dear Lord, I know it's OK to feel anger. But if I hang on to it, suppress it, or feel it over and over again, it sours me and my relationships. I want to turn my resentments over to you, today. Amen.

A final thought:
Being indecisive can lead to trouble. Think of what happens to a centipede who can't decide which foot to put forward first.

— RHR

As you read this piece, imagine your own life, having telling rings, like that of a tree trunk.

> *The tree leaves its natural record. When it dies or is cut down and one cuts at right angles to the trunk, the record of the tree's life is revealed. The rings of the tree are its living journal, written into its very fibre. These tree-ring records are so accurate that we can date pieces of wood found in charred posts and deserted buildings to the very year in which the tree was cut down. The tree records all the major events of its life. It records its births and death. All the great storms are shown in the rings, as are the droughts and the rainless and joyless years. And then there were the years growth was full and rich. The rain and sun were present along with gentle breezes.*
>
> *Nature writes the record in the tree . . .*
>
> — Morton T. Kelsey
> *Adventure Inward*
> Augsburg, 1980. p. 89

Psalm 52:8
> *But I am like a green olive tree*
> *in the house of God.*
> *I trust in the steadfast love of God*
> *for ever and ever.*

Prayer:
> Dear Lord,
> As my rings also show times of
> drought
> joy
> wind
> richness
> death
> Love me thru and thru. Amen.

Final thought:
> Everyone is a fool at least five minutes a day. Wisdom consists in not exceeding the limit.

— RHR

Let's get quiet for a minute . . . as we think about some things together:

> Mark Twain, in a whimsical mood, made this wise observation:
>> "Let us endeavor so to live that when we come to die, even the undertaker will be sorry."
>
> People who are missed most when they die are usually those who have sincerely tried to make the world better for their being in it, rather than those who have taken much out of life . . . and put little in. Those who have tried to enrich the world — to serve others — to help humanity — have their wealth within and take it with them when they die. Even in this life, those who love all are beloved by all. They really begin their heaven on earth.

As we think about this today, read Matthew 16:25.
For whoever would save his life will lose it, and whoever loses his life for my sake, will find it.

A question for discussion, or for your inner self. (optional)
Recall someone whom you respect and admire because of their "giving-of-themselves" spirit.

Here's a prayer:
O God, teach us to understand that it is by giving that we receive. Amen.

A final thought:
"All 'marriages' are happy . . . it's the living together afterwards that's rough!"

Thanks for sharing these moments. And until next time . . . be of good cheer. Peace, friend.

— RKP

Let's get quiet for a moment, as we think about some things.

Here's a story that many have encouraged me to put on the Warm-Line: My daily telephone devotional:

> *One night I dreamed I was walking along the beach with the Lord. Scenes from my life flashed across the sky. In each I noticed footprints on the sand. Sometimes there were two sets of footprints, other times there was only one.*
>
> *During the low periods of my life I could see only one set, so I said, "You promised me, Lord, that You would walk with me always. Why, when I needed You the most, have You not been there for me?"*
>
> *The Lord replied, "The times when you have seen only one set of prints, my child, is when I carried you."* *

That truly is a great story, filled with strength. And as we reflect on it now, read Psalm 28:9.

O save thy people, and bless thy
    heritage;
be thou their shepherd, and
    carry them for ever.

A question for reflection:
    As you look back on your life, do you recall a time when you were "carried" by God?

Here's a prayer:
    O God, thanks for the poets, musicians and story tellers of world. They are truly one of Your ways of "carrying" us along. Amen.

A final thought:
    "If you actually look like your passport photo, you aren't well enough to travel."

Have a nourishing day!

— RKP

---

*The origin of this story is obscure. I have seen it printed many places.

A while ago, a severe hurricane threatened the homes in a Massachusetts coastal town. Ominous radio warnings gave everyone some uneasy hours. As the sky darkened and the wind rose, one family huddled together in their home. Suddenly, with a loud crash, the power failed. In the darkness you could hear the children's muffled sobs.

"You might just as well calm down," mother said to them, trying to sound matter-of-fact. "After all, there's nothing we can do about it."

"Mother," said the youngest, "I know there's nothing we can do about *it*. But isn't there something we can do about *us*?"

Who said adults are more practical than children? They often know better than anyone what is needed.

Recall a time when you've been surprised by a child's wisdom and helpful practicality.

Luke 2:46
After three days they found him in the temple, sitting among the teachers, listening to them and asking them questions.

Prayer:
Dear Lord, grant me the serenity to accept the things I cannot change, the courage to change the things I can, and the wisdom to know the difference. Amen.

Final thought:
A gardener is someone who believes that what goes down, must come up.

— RHR

Broken Shell

My smallest and last child smashed the shell
That had been given me when I was a child:
So long, so carefully kept: a pearl shell
That filled my adult hand, its immaculate
Inner dome flushed with miniature rainbows:
A tiny cave carved in far-off seas
Whose dazzle of sun-struck gold-green
Here incredibly fixed; and the sound of seas
Which was, I grew to learn, my pulse's sound.
Now dropped and broken by that child of mine
Too young to know what he has destroyed;
Too young to tell me what I should have known.

— *Change of Weather*
Winfield Townley Scott
Doubleday and Co., Inc. 1964

Have you ever had something precious broken by someone you love? Do you remember your feelings?

Maybe that's a little like how God felt when his precious Son was broken and killed by people he loved.

John 3:16
For God so loved the world that he gave his only Son . . .

Prayer:
Dear Lord, there are things I value. But help me never to let these things become more important than any person or you. Amen.

Final thought:
It's funny that "being in hot water" usually means trouble, but being out of it is the most miserable thing that can happen to you when you're in the shower.

— RHR

Henri Nowen says that sometimes the most important gift you can give a person, is to simply receive him. Here's a story that brings that deep truth home. A man writes . . .

> Bob Griese, famed quarterback of the Miami Dolphins, was signing autographs for fans at the team's training site. Standing to one side, admiring the gracious way Griese handled the chore, I was approached by a seven- or eight-year-old boy who politely asked to borrow my pen. I watched as the youngster dug a crumpled scrap of paper from his jeans, joined the crowd and finally received the prized signature.
>
> After returning my pen with a polite "Thank you," the boy started to walk away. Suddenly he stopped, came back and re-borrowed the pen. Kneeling on the sidewalk, he laboriously printed the name JOHN on another crumbled piece of paper, and rejoined the group surrounding Bob Griese. When his turn came, he handed the paper to Griese. Momentarily disconcerted, Bob took it, and then beamed, obviously touched. "Why thank you, John," he said. And he smiled again.
>
> — George Mitchell

Think about how good it feels to be invited, welcomed, listened to, and in other ways received. Children seem to know how important that is better than anyone.

Mark 10:15
"Receive the kingdom of God like a child."

A prayer:
Dear Lord, give me a spirit of exchanging gifts with the people I meet. And help me to know that the best gift I can give a person is to truly receive him. Amen.

A final thought:
You are not an ugly duckling when somebody loves you.

— RHR

Let's get quiet for a moment, as we think about some things.

There are at least two kinds of people in the world. Those who say, "It's hopeless"; and those who say, "I'll try."

When we read the stories of the miracles which Jesus did, we can see that it was the person who was prepared to try who was helped.

For example, Jesus said to the paralyzed man whose friends carried him into his presence: "Take up your bed and walk" (Mark 2:11). The man might well have answered, "That is precisely what it is hopeless for me to try to do." But he did try, and the miracle happened!

There is not much as depressing and useless as saying, "It's hopeless." If we *try*, we can do so much more. And, of course, if we ask our Lord to help us try, the almost impossible can happen.

Lots to think about here. And as we do, read Mark 3:1-6.
He stretched out his hand, and it was restored. (v. 5)

A question for pondering:
Can you recall a time when you were surprised that something worked that you tried?

Here's a prayer:
O God, keep us trying. Amen.

A final thought:
"If at first you don't succeed . . . try looking in the wastebasket for the directions!"

Let's all leap into this day with a hop, a skip, a jump . . . and some heavenly class! Hello world!

— RKP

Let's get quiet for a minute . . . as we listen to a reading from Goethe, the German poet. He talks about the importance of friendship.

> *The world is so empty*
> *if one thinks only*
> *of mountains, rivers, and*
> *cities; but to know someone*
> *who thinks and feels with me,*
> *and who, though distant*
> *is close to me in spirit,*
> *this makes the earth for me*
> *an inhabited garden.*

— Quoted in *The Heart of Friendship*, Muriel James and Louis M. Savary (Harper and Row, 1976) p. 4

An inhabited garden! What warm and beautiful images such words bring forth.

I think it was Ignace Lepp who said that friendship is the highest relationship possible to our human family. Without it we are lonely people. Thank God for our friends.

Lots to think about here. And as we do, read John 15:15.
"I have called you friends . . ."

A question for discussion. (optional)
Sit back and recall a friend you had when you were about ten or twelve years old. When were you last in touch? Would a letter or phone call be something you could share with her or him today?

Here's a prayer:
O God, thanks for friends. And thank you for being a Friend. Amen.

A final thought:
"Show me someone who owns his/her own home . . . and I'll show you someone just coming out of a hardware store!"

Thanks for sharing these few minutes. Have a nourishing day and be of good cheer. Until next time, peace.

— RKP

Some thoughts on Pearl-making:

Pearls are produced when sand gets into and irritates an oyster. We too are called to be pearl-makers by making something beautiful out of the irritations that come into our lives, by making the best out of the worst!

For example, an illness or hospitalization gives us the opportunity to look inward and assess ourselves. It gives us time to reflect on our priorities. It provides the occasion to contemplate how we can improve the relationships that are important to us. It brings home the fact that we are not indispensable. That helps us put our work or daily routines back into proper perspective.

Good luck in your pearl-making!

— John E. Biegert.
Looking Up . . . While Lying Down
The Pilgrim Press, 1978, 1979,
by John E. Biegert
6th printing, September, 1981,
by the Pilgrim Press. p. 11

Romans 8:28
We know that in everything God works for good with those who love him . . .

Here's a prayer:
Dear Lord of love, sometimes my problems just need some good worked into them. And you can help. Thank you. Amen.

A final thought:
There is an identity crisis everywhere. Americans are seeking to find out who they are, where they're coming from, what they're made of — and how they can lose ten or twenty pounds of it.

— RHR

I saw a poster once with these words: "If everything is coming your way, you might be in the wrong lane." Here's a story that carries that thought further.

Three old men were sitting on the dock talking about their life accomplishments. One man said, braggingly, "I've been sailing for fifty years and never tipped over a sailboat." His friends looked at him astounded. "Man, you haven't really sailed then," they said. "If you had, you would have tipped over at least once or twice. To sail, I mean to really sail, you have to be on the edge."

Wow! and that could be applied to life, too, couldn't it . . . living deeply on the edge, with zest.

Luke 4:29
And they rose up and put him out of the city, and led him to the brow . . .

Prayer:
Dear Lord, it is more comfortable on the surface, but I would rather plunge deeper into the life and faith you've given me. Amen.

A final thought:
Golfer: "Just when I think golfing is only a game, I sink a 32-foot putt."

— RHR

55 Club Devotions
5/12/86

Creation is happening still. The Austrian Alps grow two inches a year, a star in the universe is born each day. Our neighbor had a baby girl last night, and I have grown to love a friend. Creation is happening still. Here's a poem that highlights this mysterious process.

"To Dance With the Waves!"

Like waves
*   rolling upon the shore*
Life forces
*   itself upon me,*
Sometimes gently,
*   Sometimes with*
*   harsh, hurried crashing.*

Standing immobile like a cliff
*   against the onslaught*
*   of the ocean,*
I am doomed to be shaped
*   by forces opposing me.*

*   But, ah, to dance*
with the waves, like the coastal sands,
*   shifting, drifting,*
weaving patterns from each wave
*   playing violently*
*   or softly*
*   upon me —*
This is to create
*   of my life*
*   a work of art.*

— Dwight H. Judy
Alive Now. Published by *The Upper Room*
May/June, 1981, p. 29. Vol. II, No. 3

Genesis 1:1
In the beginning, God created the heavens and the earth . . .

Prayer:
   O God of shapes and sizes and raw materials,
   It's remarkable the way you make and remake me,
     create and recreate.
   Thanks for the joy of that happening in my life. Amen.

Final thought:
   You can put a smile on the face of the earth by wearing one on your own.

— RHR

Here is a story of ordinary yet magnificent thoughtfulness.

For almost a year, an eighty-year-old man made a daily twenty mile trip to be with his wife, who was in a nursing home. The trip involved about two hours of bus travel each way, but he didn't mind. Always warm and outgoing, he had struck up a friendship with the bus driver and enjoyed the company of other passengers.

One day, he was standing at the bus stop in a pouring rain when a little Volkswagon pulled up and a young man called out that he had come to take him home. He went on to explain that the bus had broken down and that the driver, a friend of his, had phoned to ask if he would go to that bus stop and see that the elderly man waiting there got home safely.

Isn't that kind of helping a beautiful thing?

Mark 9:41
"... *whoever gives you a cup of cold water to drink* ..."

Prayer:
Dear Lord, thank you for people who are thoughtful, when it would be easier to just not remember. Amen.

Final thought:
Ahhh, the jet age. Breakfast in Paris, dinner in Hong Kong, luggage in Seattle.

— RHR

Let's get quiet for a minute, as we reflect on these thoughts of Harriet du Autermont: She calls this "Some Faith at Any Cost."

> *No vision and you perish;*
> *No ideal, and you're lost;*
> *Your heart must ever cherish*
> *Some faith at any cost.*
>
> *Some hope, some dream to cling to,*
> *Some rainbow in the sky,*
> *Some melody to sing to,*
> *Some service that is high.*

Isn't that great! I love it! I love it! And as we think about it, read Hebrews 11:1.
> *Now faith is the assurance of things hoped for, the conviction of things not seen.*

A question for discussion:
What would be one of your definitions of "Faith?"

Here's a prayer:
O God, help us to keep the faith! Amen.

A final thought:
"When we were borrowing our customs from older cultures, who was the idiot who passed up the siesta?"

Thanks for sharing these few moments. And until next time . . . peace.

— RKP

Let's get quiet for a moment as we reflect on some things.

Here's a thought from Helen Keller:

> *There are red-letter days in our lives when we meet people who thrill us like a fine poem, people whose handshake is brimful of unspoken sympathy, and whose sweet, rich natures impart to our eager, impatient spirits a wonderful restfulness which, in its essence, is divine.*
>
> *The perplexities, irritations, and worries that have absorbed us pass like unpleasant dreams, and we wake to see with new eyes and hear with new ears the beauty and harmony of God's real world.*

Lots to think about here. And as we do, read Proverbs 17:17.
A friend loves at all times, and a brother (sister) is born for adversity.

A question to ponder:
Recall someone whom you are almost always happy to see.

Here's a prayer:
O God, help us to *really* hear and see. Amen.

A final thought:
"The only job where you start at the top is . . . digging a hole."

Have a nourishing day!

— RKP

A woman opened a box which contained her new, unassembled bamboo blinds. In it she found yards of rope and dozens of hooks and loops. The only instructions were: "If you do not use everything in this package, the blind will not work."

That's a lot of help, isn't it?

Another man bought a plastic chair in the local supermarket. On the packaging was this warning: "Do Not Sit in Chair Without Being Fully Assembled."

A lot of things in life don't work as they should, simply because we haven't taken the time to organize and assemble in the proper way. This could apply to our job, family, day, too. Sometimes we try to put things together in a way that won't fit, and other times we may even be missing some of the parts.

Read Matthew 19:22 and around there:
When the young man heard this he went away sorrowful; for he had great possessions.

Prayer:
Dear Lord, I've tried to put my life together on my own. It hasn't worked. I'm ready to begin being assembled by you and your loving creative power. Amen.

A final thought:
Friendship is born at that moment when one person says to another, "What! You, too? I thought I was the only one."
— C. S. Lewis

— RHR

A father who works with mathematical statistics in his job, on a Saturday afternoon, agreed to look after his four small and energetic children while his wife went shopping. He had never taken care of them alone before. When she returned, he gave her this note.

"Dried tears — 11 times. Tied shoelaces — 15 times. Blew up toy balloons — 5 per child. Average life of each balloon — 10 seconds. Warned children not to run across street — 26 times. Children insisted on running across street — 26 times. Number of Saturdays I will go through this again — 0."

Come on, Dad, hang in there.

Psalm 103:1
Bless the Lord, O my soul, and all that is in me, bless His holy name.

Prayer:
Dear Lord, thank you for the beautiful day and the, at least for now, good feeling of well-being. Amen.

A final thought:
Snow is the peanut butter of nature. It's crunchy, kids love it, and it sticks to the roof of your house.

— RHR

Let's get quiet for a minute . . . as we think about some things.

> I remember writing a note to our Mayor when we lived in Salt Lake City. I thanked him for his position on a rather difficult issue. Almost immediately a reply came back saying, "Many of my letters come from folks complaining about this or that, but yours is only about the 3rd or 4th letter of appreciation I've gotten in my eight years in office."
>
> And then there's the story of the old Vermont farmer who, on reflecting on forty years of marriage, told his wife, "You know, Martha, sometimes I love you so much it's all I can do to keep from telling you."
>
> We smile at that, yet how sad. How often we let the opportunity go by to drop a golden nugget of praise or appreciation or love into the life of another simply through reluctance or negligence. We fail to nourish that life with a little encouragement, and our own lives with joy and thanks. Is today the day *you* need to send a note or make a phone call or give someone a great big hug?

Lots to ponder here! And as we do, read Galatians 5:22.
But the fruit of the Spirit is . . . joy.

A question for thought and discussion:
> When was the last time you wrote a note to (or called) someone and let her know how much you appreciated something she did?

Here's a prayer:
> O God, where there is darkness . . . bring light. Amen.

A final thought:
> "Things ain't what they used to be . . . and probably never was."
>
> — Will Rogers

Have a nourishing day!

— RKP

Let's get quiet for a minute . . . as we ponder some things.

One of my friends shared this with me recently. It's called "Rainbows in a Friend."

> *The storm had surfaced*
> *Winds of pain against sail*
> *I pushed on tired and ill*
> *Against the mighty gale*
>
> *Strength had withered in me*
> *Alas, I thought I would end*
> *But the clouds disappeared*
> *In the guise of a friend*
>
> *A friend that prayed with me*
> *A friend that believed as I*
> *That God controlled my vessel*
> *And the tears in my eyes*
>
> *We sailed the calm water*
> *The sun God did send*
> *Along with His rainbow*
> *That I found in a friend*

— Marilyn Verbitsky,
Unpublished Poem. Used by permission

As we ponder this thought, read St. John 15:15.
". . . I have called you friends."

A question to ponder:
What is a good definition of a friend?

Here's a prayer:
O God, thank you for Rainbows called Friends. Amen.

A final thought:
Despite all the talk about the speed of supersonic transports, no engineer has ever been able to concoct anything that can go faster than a vacation.

Thanks for your presence today. Until next time . . . be of good cheer. And be careful today.

— RKP

Newness can be frightening and exhilarating at the same time. Here's a poem by Robin E. Van Cleef that captures some of that mixture.

Birthright

What new thing have you for me today, Lord?
  A new song?
    A new thought?
      A new hope?
        A new birth?

There was a time when I embraced the dawn,
  Reveling in life,
    Enjoying each new day,
      Savoring each experience.
But now I play the old nostalgia game,
cluttering my soul with time-locked trivia.

Why am I frightened by your newness,
fearing your cleansing, liberating wind
  that makes life new?
Can I, once grown, begin to grow again?

I come now in the nighttime of my soul
  seeking the dawn, the birth.

— *Alive Now*
March/April, 1981. p. 33

When someone says "new things can be frightening," what does that mean to you?

Psalm 51:10
  Create in me a clean heart
  and put a new and right spirit within me.

Prayer:
  Dear Lord, I feel so old and stuffy today. Put some of your freshness back in me. Amen.

Final thought:
  The surest way to get down to the real nitty-gritty is to eat a peanut butter and jelly sandwich, at the beach.

— RHR

Think about your parents as you reflect on this story. Do you remember the support they gave you? Let this woman's experience trigger some feelings within you.

> To be at work on time after a snowstorm, I decided to catch the day's first bus. Standing in the blowing snow at a bus stop a block away from me were an elderly man and woman. When the bus appeared, its driver, with a toot of the horn and a wave of the hand, passed right by the waving couple.
>
> I was shocked by his rudeness, and when he stopped for me, I angrily asked him why he had left those two people standing in the cold. "That's my mom and dad," he explained with a grin. "I just started on the job today."
>
> — Edna Baker

Philemon 7
For I have derived much joy and comfort from your love . . .

Here's a prayer:
Father, I thank you for my parents. They've never quit supporting and loving me. Amen.

A final thought:
Nothing makes one feel at home like a great snowstorm.

— RHR

Let's get quiet for a minute as we reflect on these words of Dr. Patricia Beatty. They were first shared by her at a meeting of both "Disabled" and "Abled" people in Fargo on November 6, 1981. I was moved by them at that time, and I still am.

A Tribute
(To many in the audience, by those of us who are handicapped)

Thank you
> *For taking the time*
>> *To help me when I need it and for waiting when I can do it myself*
>> *To listen on my hard days*
>> *To laugh, cry, talk and be with me as a friend*

Thank you
> *For acknowledging my worth as a person*
>> *By depending on me when you have a problem*
>> *By seeing, using and valuing my abilities in spite of my disabilities*
>> *By sharing life with me as an equal — in little things and big things*

Thank you
> *For being honest and direct with me with your frustrations, anger and disappointments, and letting me share mine*

Thank you
> *For recognizing my worth as a unique person who can both touch and be touched, love and be loved. Who can contribute to society and to a life together.*

Although being disabled can be and often is difficult, so can being healthy, if you are alone. Special friends, be they husband, sister, daughter, teacher, nurse or neighbor, are important to everyone. Thank you for being special to me.

Wow! Lots to ponder here. And as we do, read 2 Samuel 4:4, and around there.
> *Jonathan, the son of Saul, had a son . . . His nurse took him up . . . and, as she fled in her haste, he fell, and became lame. And his name was Mephibosheth.*

A question for discussion:
    How do you feel when you are around someone with a disabling condition . . . say, someone in a wheelchair?

Here's a prayer:
    O God, thank you for the critical intervention of the right friend, the right book, the right thought . . . at precisely the right time. Amen.

A final thought:
    "Remember when . . . health foods were whatever your mother said you'd better eat . . . or else!?"

— RKP

A cement contractor who does a lot of business with mobile-home-park residents tells this story. Apparently, many of the leisure-conscious retirees order green cement "lawns" so that they no longer have to mow grass and pull weeds.

Most customers are happy with their no-care yards, but one man called to express dissatisfaction. The contractor drove out to the mobile-home park, but could find no apparent cause for complaint. In fact, "I hate to brag," he said to the man, "but this cement looks as good as on the day I poured it."

"That's the trouble," groaned the man. "It's *too* perfect, and it's getting on my nerves. I want you to paint a dandelion right in the middle."

Anything that appears to be perfect in the world is also probably artificial, and thereby also out of touch with our deepest human existence and need.

What are some artificial items and products you despise?

Genesis 11:4
   . . . let us make a name for ourselves.

Ecclesiastes 3:14
   I know that whatever God does endures forever: nothing can be added to it, nor anything taken from it: God has made it so, in order that men should fear before him.

Prayer:
   Dear Lord, save us from artificiality and other towers of Babel. Amen.

Final thought:
   It's a good thing God accepts us as we are, because we sure change slowly.

   — Ron Rude (while playing tennis)

— RHR

Here's a poem that helps me see some of the wideness and beauty of the earth and life.

> *Flying, I saw vast lands:*
> *the curve of the earth, brown soil,*
> *green patches, and desert sands.*
> *Driving, I saw much more:*
> *trees, pastures, animals, houses, signs, and lakes*
> *smeared past the glass in the car door.*
> *Bicycling, I saw in detail what was smeared and vast*
> *while driving and flying over the earth so fast.*
> *Walking, I discovered that the earth had a feel*
> *that coursed through my arteries by way of my heel.*
> *Crawling, I discovered that it was hard work to see;*
> *the more I crawled the more it overwhelmed me.*
> *Stopping, I realized that I could never see*
> *everything that God had placed within one foot of me.*
>
> — Howard Pillot, from *Power* Magazine
> Vol. 40, No. 1, Fall, 1981, p. 24
> Published by Christian Youth Publications
> Box 734, St. Charles, Missouri 63310

Isn't that an imaginative, soul-stretching writing? The poet, Howard Pillot, is a young high school student. What a wide-open eye for the dimensions of God's creation.

The Psalmist also had a wide eye for God and his world when over twenty-seven centuries ago, he wrote:

> *O lord, how manifold are thy works!*
> *In wisdom has thou made them all;*
> *The earth is full of thy creatures.*
>
> Psalm 104:24

Here's a prayer:
> Dear Lord, there's a whole world out there and very near. Open all my senses and my mind and heart so that I can take in a good chunk of creation and you. Amen.

A final thought:
> Even age doesn't diminish the extreme disappointment of having a scoop of ice cream fall off your cone, onto the floor.

— RHR

Here's a thought for when we take ourselves too seriously.

> *Carol Burnett's oldest child is named Carrie. When Carrie was seven, she was naughty one day and Carol gave her a spanking. "At bedtime she was still sniffling," Carol recalls. "So I went in and put my arms around her, saying, 'Now, you know I love you very much.' And then I talked about character and what she did that was wrong, and she listened, never taking her eyes from my face. I began congratulating myself — boy, you are really getting through, she'll remember this when she's 40.*
>
> *"I talked for 20 minutes. Carrie was spellbound; we were practically nose to nose. As I paused, searching for the clincher, Carrie asked, 'Mommy, how many teeth do you have?'"*

Beautiful.

1 Corinthians 8:2
> *If anyone imagines that he learns something, he does not yet know as he ought to know.*

Prayer:
> Dear Lord, when I take myself and what I know too seriously, thank you for children who gently disarm my loftiness. Amen.

A final thought:
> Occasionally a day comes along that is so beautiful, you hope it is the pilot episode for a continuing series.
> — Bill Vaughan

— RHR

Let's get quiet for a minute, as we think about some things together.

> On November 10, 1979, I buried one of the members of our congregation. She was ninety-four years old. Fiercely independent, she had found it necessary to spend the last few years of her life in a nursing care center. It wasn't easy for her at first. The following note was found among her things after her death. It was passed to her from one of the other residents:
>
> > *Mali, I wish we were young again*
> > *so I could be with you*
> > *So we could walk to the setting sun*
> > *Holding our hands when day is done.*
>
> Isn't that great! Isn't that fine! How grand that Mali and her friend could feel a glimpse of real friendship and love, even (maybe especially) in their later years.

Lots to think about here. And as we do, read 1 Corinthians 13:8, and around there.
Love never ends . . .

A question to think about:
If you were young again, what would you do differently?

Here's a prayer:
O God, thank you for stout promises and bright hopes that keep us thinking kindly of the future . . . with love. Amen.

A final thought:
"What most persons consider as virtue . . . after the age of forty is simply a loss of energy!"

Have a nourishing day.

— RKP

Let's get quiet for a moment as we think about some things.

What is friendship anyhow? One person put it this way. I found this beautiful saying on a greeting card:

> *Friendship is a special blessing*
>   *from above.*
> *It's the sharing of activities*
>   *with someone who understands and cares.*
> *It's a warm ray of sunshine that fills*
>   *our hearts in times of need. It's the*
>   *bringing out of beautiful things*
>   *in each other that no one*
>   *else looked hard enough to find.*
> *It's the mutual trust and honesty*
>   *that lets us be ourselves at all times.*
>
> — Iverson Williams

Lots to think about here. And as we do, read Psalm 55:13.
> But it is you, my equal,
>   my companion, my familiar friend.

A question to consider:
> Someone has said, "A friend is someone who knows all about you . . . and still likes you." What would be your description or definition of a friend?

Here's a prayer:
> O God, thank you that friends are forever! Amen.

A final thought:
> To get maximum attention . . . it's hard to beat a good, big, fat mistake!

Be of good cheer.

— RKP

Here's a story to trigger some memories.

> There was a family who always had trouble on vacations. Each year they would get about seventy-five miles out of town, and Mom would cry, "Oh, no! I left the iron on." Each year they would turn and go back. But it was never plugged in.
>
> One time the carload was headed for Yellowstone National Park and, sure enough, almost to the mile marker, Mom gasped, "I just know I left the iron on." Her husband didn't say a word. He just pulled over, got out, opened the trunk and handed her the iron. And every year after that, he made sure that the iron was in the trunk before they left on vacation.

Recall something that always happened on your vacations as a child. Does the memory make you smile?

Psalm 106:1
> *Praise the LORD!*
> *O Give thanks to the LORD;*
>   *for he is good;*
> *for his steadfast love endures*
>   *forever!*

Here's a prayer:
> Dear Lord, thank you for my past; it was a good training program for today. Amen.

A final thought:
> You probably wouldn't worry so much about what people think of you if you knew how seldom they do.
>
> — Olin Miller

— RHR

Let's get quiet for a moment as we ponder this piece from Robert Farley. The source of it is lost to me:

Think of the hopes that lie before you
   Not of the waste that lies behind;
Think of the treasures you have gathered,
   Not the ones you failed to find;
Think of the service you may render,
   Not of serving self alone;
Think of the happiness of others,
   And in this you'll find your own.

Good words for us all. As we think about them, read Matthew 10:39.
   He who finds his life will lose it, and he who loses his life for my sake will find it.

A question to mull over:
   What is one thing you could do for another today that would surprise and please that person?

Here's a prayer:
   O God, keep us looking forward . . . with lots of hope Amen.

A final thought:
   "How long a minute is . . . depends on which side of the bathroom door you are on!"

May your day be filled with every good thing. And peace, friend.

— RKP

Put everything away for a moment, except this page, and think along with me.

A friend sent me this piece in the mail some time back. It had been helpful to her when her mother was very ill. She didn't give the source of it but it is too good not to pass along. So here goes:

> *God hath not promised*
>   *Skies always blue,*
> *Flower-strewn pathways*
>   *All our lives through;*
> *God hath not promised*
>   *Sun without rain,*
> *Joy without sorrow,*
>   *Peace without pain.*
>
> *But God hath promised*
>   *Strength for the day,*
> *Rest for the labor,*
>   *Light for the way.*
> *Grace for the trials,*
>   *Help from above,*
> *Unfailing sympathy*
>   *Undying love . . .*

— Selected

Lots to think about here. And as we do, read Lamentations 3:22-23.
The steadfast love of the Lord never ceases,
his mercies never come to an end;
they are new every morning.

A question to consider:
How could you put the thought of the poem above into one sentence in your own words?

Here's a prayer:
O God, you are the wellspring of every good thing. Make us your servants. Amen.

A final thought:
Remember: "If you cross your bridges before you come to them . . . you have to pay the toll twice!"

May you always feel God's nourishment in the problems and graces of your life.

— RKP

Read this story with an open mind.

> *Together we ride up in the hills behind our house.*
> *She's the one who taught me how to ride.*
> *I said I was too old to learn,*
> *but she ignored that,*
> *and with logic,*
> *drove right through my weak defenses*
> *til I opened up my mind*
> *and now I ride.*
> *Because those clear, unclouded eyes saw through me,*
> *I know a whole new world*
> *I might have missed.*
> *And I also know the joy it is*
> *to have a daughter*
> *who is also*
> *a good friend.*
>
> — Raphael Marie Turnbull
> *Woman to Woman*
> 1979. Published by Raphael Marie Turnbull and
> The C. R. Gibson Company

Maybe our pride does too often and too rapidly dismiss the suggestions and wisdom of others. Perhaps we would do well to listen to and even try what others have found truly exciting or helpful.

Proverbs 8:33
Hear instruction and be wise,
and do not neglect it.

Prayer:
Dear Lord,
Thank you for ministering to me
through songs
through sunsets
through symbols
and even through other people's suggestions. Amen.

Final thought:
Sometimes the best helping hand you can get is a good firm push.

— JoAnn Thomas

— RHR

People who smile a lot and are genuine are fun to be around. They can light up a room or a day. Josh Billings shares this piece entitled "Funny Face."

> There is one kind of laugh that I always did recommend; it looks out of the eye first with a merry twinkle, then it creeps down on its hands and knees and plays around the mouth like a pretty moth around the blaze of a candle, then it steals over into the dimples of the cheeks and rides around in those little whirlpools for a while, then it lights up the whole face like the mellow bloom on a damask rose, then it swims up on on the air with a peal as clear and as happy as a dinner bell, then it goes back again on golden tiptoe like an angel out for an airing, and lies down on its little bed of violets in the heart where it came from.

Luke 6:21
"Blessed are you that weep now, for you shall laugh."

Prayer:
Dear Lord,
Thanks for laughter
which is good for my heart
and face. Amen.

A final thought:
Bringing up children is like holding a very wet bar of soap — too firm a grasp and it shoots from your hand, too loose a grasp and it slides away. A gentle but firm grasp keeps it in your control.

— RHR

Let's get quiet for a moment, as we think about some things.

> Some days are harder than others. I hope your day is going OK for you. But, if not . . . Here's a thought that may help:

> > *God's strength behind you,*
> > *His concern for you,*
> > *His love within you, and*
> > *His arms beneath you are*
> > > *more than sufficient for*
> > > > *the job ahead of you.*
> > > > > — William Arthur Ward*

Lots to ponder here. And as we do, read Psalm 46:1.
God is our refuge and strength, a very present help in trouble.

A question for discussion: (optional)
Do you remember a time when God seemed especially close to you? Share it if you would like to.

Here's a prayer:
O God, thanks for your continued presence. Amen.

A final thought:
"A well-adjusted person is one who makes the same mistake twice . . . without getting nervous!"

Thanks for sharing these moments with me. Until next time, be of good cheer. And peace, my friend.

— RKP

*Found on a banner in a church in North Dakota.

Let's get quiet for a minute, as we listen to a reading from Gerhard Frost. It's called "My Soul Waits."

> *There must be dry times;*
> *all living things must wait*
> *and be tested.*
> *All things that grow*
> *share one secret,*
> *the mystery of hidden pain.*
>
> *The grain of wheat*
> *must suffer early season dryness,*
> *those miniature droughts,*
> *not too long, but real.*
> *They make for depth*
> *through struggle.*
>
> *Young roots must **reach***
> *lest shallow-rooted greenness*
> *prove insufficient to the harvest.*
>
> *I, too, struggle*
> *to reach deeper.*
> *I'm afraid, Lord, afraid*
> *of being too much surface*
> *with insufficient depth.*
> *I suffer the dry times.*
> *My soul awaits the rain.*
>
> *The secret of the wheat field*
> *is my secret, too.*
>
> — *Homing: In the Presence*
> (Winston, 1978) p. 21

Wow! Lots to think about here. And as we do, read Psalm 46:10.
Be still, and know that I am God.

A question for discussion. (optional)
Can you recall a "dry" time in your life? What did it feel like?

Here's a prayer:
O God, give us depth . . . and help us with our patience. Amen.

A final thought:
> "Some people are like blotters . . . soak it all up but get it all backward!"

Thanks for sharing these few moments. And until next time . . . peace.

— RKP

Think of a conversation you had today. How would you describe what took place?

> *When Webster's Third New International Dictionary-Unabridged was published in 1961, the editor-in-chief wrote a lengthy introduction to the volume which included this remarkable statement: "It is now fairly clear that before the 20th century is over every community in the world will have learned how to communicate with all the rest of humanity."*
>
> *That certainly will be a glorious day! I must confess to being not nearly so optimistic as the editor-in-chief of Webster's. In fact, what seems to me to be "now fairly clear" is that people who already use the same dictionary, even members of the same household, find communication difficult at best and, at times, impossible.*
>
> — David E. Babin
> Week In — Week Out
> Seabury 1976 p. 11

Question to ponder:
What kind of "attitudes" facilitate healthy communication? How important is listening?

Proverbs 18:2
*A fool takes no pleasure in understanding,
but only in expressing his opinion.*

Prayer:
Dear Lord,
Communication is part of our nature,
basic to our most joyful triumphs and
lingering troubles.
Help us to listen and talk better. Amen.

A final thought:
Never talk down to your children; they may mimic you to their peers after.

— Robert Eddy

— RHR

Here's a poem I wrote following a conversation with a good friend.

Some Hurts

Some hurts don't heal
you just learn to live with them
and that stands to reason
if you loved someone enough
and now they're gone.

Some hearts don't mend
though, scabs and scar tissue form
and new relationships
fill part of the void
but, oh, the void is great.

Some lives won't ever be whole
like before
yet, they probably weren't so even then
it just seems like it now
looking back.

Some hurts don't heal
you just learn to live with them.

O God,
help me to live with that.
Amen.

— Ronald Rude

I've learned that following the death of a close friend or family member, it takes a good year, or more to even begin to feel "normal" again. Has that been your experience?

Matthew 2:18
> *A voice was heard in Ramah, wailing and loud lamentation, Rachel weeping for her children; she refused to be consoled, because they were no more.*

Prayer:
> Life is a combination of fullness and emptiness. Help me to see your presence in both. Amen.

A final thought:
> "Stay" is a charming word in the vocabulary of friendship.

— RHR

Let's get quiet for a minute or so, as we think about a few things.

Vincent Van Gogh said this:
> *Love is something eternal — the aspects may change, but not the essence. There is the same difference in a person before and after he is in love as there is in an unlighted lamp and one that is burning. The lamp was there and it is a good lamp, but now it is shedding light, too, and that is its real function.*

Lots to ponder here. And as we do, read 1 John 4:7-8.
> *"Beloved, let us love one another; for love is of God, and he who loves is born of God and knows God. He who does not love does not know God; for God is love."*

Here's a question to chew on:
> How would you describe "love"?

Here's a prayer:
> O God, we feel your presence . . . through others. Thank you for those we love and those who love us. Amen.

A final thought:
> Something to think about while in the daily traffic jam:
>> "Wherever the place,
>> Whatever the time,
>> Every lane moves
>> But the one where I'm."

Be of good cheer today. And be careful out there.

— RKP

Let's get quiet for a moment as we think about some things.

Here's a reading from Rod McKuen:

> *Clouds are not*
> *the cheeks of angels*
> > *you know*
> *they're only clouds.*
> > *Friendly sometimes,*
> *but you can never be sure.*
> *If I had longer arms*
> *I'd push the clouds away*
> *or make them hang*
> > *above the water*
> > > *somewhere else,*
> *but I'm just a man*
> *who needs and wants,*
> *mostly things he'll never have.*
> *Looking for that thing*
> *that's hardest to find —*
> > *himself.*

— *Seasons in the Sun*
Pocket Books, Division of Simon and Schuster,
630 Fifth Avenue
New York, New York 10020, p. 39

Lots to think about here. And as we do, read Mark 8:36.
For what does it profit a person, to gain the whole world and forfeit his life?

A question for discussion or reflection:
When you think of clouds, what words or thoughts come to your mind? Did you ever lie on your back and look at the clouds and imagine the different shapes as things you recognized?

Here's a prayer:
O God, help us to find meaning in all we do. Amen.

A final thought:
"Show me a squirrel's home and I'll show you a nutcracker's suite."

Be of good cheer.

— RKP

I saw a sign on the window of a paint store recently, which said,

> The next time you think a gallon of paint costs too much, remember that:
> — 6 ounces of Right Guard sells for $2.97 or $57.40 a gallon.
> — ½ ounce of nail polish sells for $3.00 or $768 a gallon.
> — .2 ounce of Binaca Mouth Spray sells for $1.67 or $1,280 a gallon.

Nail polish lasts several days.
Right Guard and Binaca last several hours.
But paint lasts several years.

Paint is still the best buy in town.

We can say the same about other things in life, can't we? . . . like love, faith, hope, truth. They still go a long way and last a long time.

Recall something that has lasted for a long time in your life. Of what significance has it been for you?

1 Corinthians 13:13
So faith, hope, love abide; these three; but the greatest of these is love.

Prayer:
Dear Lord,
Help me to love,
to make it a priority,
something I value in life.
You've made me a priority in your being
and with your help
I'll last. Amen.

A final thought:
Objects are lost because people look where they are not, instead of where they are.

— RHR

Think of a pet you've had and loved in your lifetime. A man tells this story.

> When I was a small boy, I begged my father to let me have a puppy. He finally gave in, saying, "Okay, son, but you must understand that we will only take her on a trial basis, and if she doesn't work out, back she goes."
>
> Many years have gone by, and now my dog is very old. One day, as my father and the old dog walked across the yard together, I was touched to hear him say quietly to her, "Remember, you're only here on a trial basis."
>
> — Michael McCurdy

Isn't it amazing how love gets under our skin and quickly makes a remarkably strong bond, even sometimes with animals?

Song of Solomon 8:7
> *Many waters cannot quench love,*
> *neither can floods drown it.*
> *If a man offered for love*
> *all the wealth of his house,*
> *it would be utterly scorned.*

Here's a prayer:
O God, thanks for puppy love, and other important bonds. Amen.

A final thought:
Aren't people funny?
If you tell someone that there are 270,678,934,368 stars in the universe, he'll believe you — but if a sign says "Fresh Paint" that same person has to make a personal investigation.

— RHR

Let's get quiet for a moment as we think about some things.

A brief piece today from George Kelly. It's called "Finder's Keepers," and I can't locate where I first found it:

> *What a little thing makes the*
> *   world go wrong!*
> *A word too short or a smile*
> *   too long;*
> *Then comes the mist — and the*
> *   blinding rain,*
> *And life is never the same*
> *   again.*

Lot's to ponder here. And as we do, read John 11:35.
   Jesus wept.

Here's a prayer:
   O God, keep us honest, but gentle with each other. Amen.

A question to mull over:
   When was the last time you really cried?

A final thought:
   For God so loved the world . . . that he didn't send a committee.

Thanks for thinking along with me. Have a nourishing day.

— RKP

Let's get quiet for a minute as we listen to a reading from Robert Raines.

Give Me a Good Eye

Give me a good eye
to see all the cartoons people make
by being alive . . .
to delight in the vigor of young people
out to make the world,
and the twinkle in the eye of an old man
who remembers the good young days . . .

Thanks for those who love me
in the common ways of a smile,
a letter, a phone call,
and all the gentle touches
of hand and heart . . .

Thanks for those who confront me
with anger, hurt, pain,
and remind me that I don't always see them
as I go by . . .

If in pleasure we have gone our separate ways,
in pain draw us together.

— *Lord, Could You Make It a Little Better?*
(Word, 1972) p. 123

As we think about this, read Psalm 136:1
> O Give thanks to the Lord,
>> for he is good,
> for his steadfast love endures
>> for ever.

A question for discussion. (optional)
> Can you recall a time when pain drew you closer to another?

Here's a prayer:
> O God, draw us all together . . . when we have drifted apart. Amen.

A final thought:
> Many persons have gotten into trouble by not expressing themselves well. There's a world of difference between, "You look like the breath of spring," and "You look like the end of a hard winter."

— RKP

Let's get quiet for a minute . . . as we think together today.

On those days when your work seems like "trying to nail pudding to a wall" (Aetna Ad) don't fight it. Read a good poem. Here's one I read recently on a greeting card I received:

> *Climb the mountains and get*
> * their good tidings.*
> *Nature's peace will flow into you*
> * as sunshine flows into trees.*
> *The winds will blow their own freshness*
> * into you, and the storms their energy,*
> *   while cares will drop off*
> *   like autumn leaves.*
>
> — John Muir

Now . . . go for a long walk or a gentle run, and see if this poetry is true.

As we think about this, read Psalm 24:1
The earth is the Lords, and the fullness thereof.

A question to think about:
What part of nature brings refreshment to you?

Here's a prayer:
O God, thank you for the warmth of our earth. Amen.

A final thought:
A friend said, "I am a light eater. As soon as it is light, I start eating."

Thanks for sharing your presence today. And be careful out there today. Shalom, friend.

— RKP

"Let It Be Forgotten"

Let it be forgotten, as a flower is forgotten,
 Forgotten as a fire that once was singing gold,
Let it be forgotten for ever and ever,
 Time is a kind friend, he will make us old.

If anyone asks, say it was forgotten
 Long and long ago,
As a flower, as a fire, as a hushed footfall
 In a long forgotten snow.

> — From *Collected Poems*
> by Sara Teasdale
> The MacMillan Co. 1920
> Found in *American Verse*,
> Edited by Oscar Williams.
> Pocket Books. 1972. p. 468

We can't forget our grudges, they're too strong. But we can let them be forgotten, by letting God have them. Let go and let God.

Read Psalm 130:4
 But there is forgiveness with thee, that thou mayest be feared.

Here's a prayer:
 Create in me a clean heart, O God, and put a new and right spirit within me. Amen.

A final thought:
 Winter storms aren't getting any worse, it's just that there are more things that won't work during them.

— RHR

> ". . . and I don't care if I ever see you again! Do you hear me?!" Lucy leaves, Linus enters. "She really hurt your feelings, didn't she, Charlie Brown? I hope she didn't take all the life out of you."
>
> "No, not completely," replies Charlies Brown. "But you can number me among the walking wounded!"
>
> — A *Peanuts* Comic Strip
> by Charles Schultz

I have a picture in one of my books of a little girl crying. Actually, she's not crying yet. The tears are under control. But the eyes are definitely moist, and the face quivered, and deep sobs are about to burst forth from the deep.

Her picture makes me wonder . . . What makes this little one so sad? There's hurt in her eyes. But not the kind that comes from a broken toy, or skinned knee, or even a hungry stomach. No, her wound speaks of rejection. Someone she loves doesn't want her. Someone she enjoys being with hasn't the time. Someone she's tried to please won't notice.

How awful to be rejected at her age or at any age.

Proverbs 3:27
> *Do not withhold good from those to
>   whom it is due,
> when it is in your power to do it.*

Here's a prayer:
> Dear Lord, open my ears and heart to people who have experienced rejection way too often. Amen.

A final thought:
> God's paint will stick only if the surface has been roughed up a bit, the shiny substance sanded off, wax and grease removed, even old paint (old understandings of God) scraped away.
>
> — Ronald Rude
> while painting

—RHR